D0383823

Striking
Sails

A Pastoral-Psychological View of Growing Older in Our Society

translated from the Dutch by

Kenneth R. Mitchell

Abingdon Press
Nashville

STRIKING SAILS
A Pastoral-Psychological View of Growing Older in Our Society

Originally published as *De Zeilen Strijken:* Over het ouder worden © 1980
Gooi en Sticht, Hilversum as ISBN 90 304 0183 4

Library of Congress Cataloging in Publication Data

Faber, Heije, 1907–
Striking sails.
Translation of: De zeilen strijken.
Bibliography: p.
1. Church work with the aged. 2. Aged—Religious
life. 3. Aged—Netherlands. I. Title.
BV4435.F3213 1984 261.8'3426 83-15033

ISBN 0-687-39941-6

MANUFACTURED BY THE PARTHENON PRESS AT
NASHVILLE, TENNESSEE, UNITED STATES OF AMERICA

Contents

Striking
Sails

Translator's Preface

In translating the work of a friend, one becomes even more aware than usual of the truth of the Italian pun/proverb, *tradittore, traduttore,* "the translator is a traitor." It is never quite possible to render into another language the elegance or the style of the original. The present book grew out of a series of lectures given by Professor Faber to his students in Tilburg; it therefore alternates between a chatty style and an erudite, formal style. One can almost hear the writer carefully making a complex point but then rounding it off with a casual illustration. I have tried to preserve that style in this translation.

Professor Faber's illustrations often involve Dutch places and organizations. At times, I have added to the translated text the name of an American location that in my opinion would convey the approximate flavor of the original Dutch locale. Where he mentions organizations peculiar to the Netherlands, I have substituted the name of a comparable organization in the U.S.A.

There are also one or two places where there is simply no acceptable English translation of a particular Dutch word or phrase. At such a point the translator's job is to convey the content and feeling tone of the original in any way that makes sense in English.

In these days of consciousness about gender inclusive and gender exclusive language, it quickly becomes apparent that each language (and each culture) is at a different stage of awareness. Usage in the Netherlands when this book was originally published involved the exclusive use of masculine pronouns whenever the antecedent was general. "The pastor" is, linguistically at least, presumed to be male, although there are certainly female pastors in some Dutch churches. I have followed the usage of the original with some reluctance. The various usages such as "he/she" and the alternation of masculine and feminine pronouns from occurrence to occurrence or chapter to chapter are all unpleasantly cumbersome. Let the reader be aware that both the original author and the translator are well aware of the fact that both humanity in general and the ranks of ordained clergy contain both men and women.

The final problem has to do with citations and references. The original text and notes do not contain the names of publishers, but only of the city and date of the publication. In addition, Professor Faber worked from Dutch, German, French, and English texts, and it is almost impossible to ascertain whether the Dutch and French books have ever appeared in English. I have therefore adopted the expedient of simply translating where it seemed important. This may leave some readers with a bit of irritation where a Dutch, German, or French title is stuck in the text of the book. To the best of my knowledge, all titles available in English are so indicated in the notes or in the bibliography.

—Kenneth R. Mitchell

1

The Old Among Us

Writing about old people carries with it certain specific difficulties. We generally attach certain images to old people, images which arouse particular feelings in us. First, then, a word about the images which arise for us in connection with the word *old*. Some examples will make clear what I intend.

Not so long ago one of my friends had his seventieth birthday. I telephoned him to wish him a happy birthday. When he came to the telephone, I could hear the background noise in the room where he picked up the phone: a happy buzz of voices. There was obviously a large and lively group with him. He himself was clearly in a good mood. "I used to have," he said, "a mental picture of a seventy-year-old as an old, crippled person, who could walk erect only with difficulty, and who had trouble speaking. But I have to speak frankly; I don't have the slightest feeling of being seventy. I still have some work to do, I play music regularly, I travel a lot. In fact, I've just come back from a visit to one of our children in the West."

My friend knew from his own experience that young men—or middle-aged ones, for that matter—possess images of old people that often bear little resemblance to the images they have of themselves. Whoever thinks about that for a few minutes must come to the conclusion that such a discrepancy is evidence of a definite alienation between generations and of an equally definite isolation of older people in our society.

I find another example in a book by H. C. Rümke entitled *Levenstijdperken van de Man.*[1] In it he writes about old age, using a striking image.

"The season is over," writes Rümke, "but he stays behind. The place is empty; many superficial acquaintances that he's made, and even many close friends, have left. With the few who remain there is an odd feeling of fellowship. He's alone; the chance to go anywhere he likes is past; he can no longer wander the whole world. After a bit of grumbling that this or that opportunity should still be open, the inexorable shrinkage is accepted. The weather becomes cooler. If up to now he has paid little attention to the water temperature—for he lives by the sea—now he has to be on the alert for good days. This accepted limitation offers, oddly enough, a feeling of peace that he never knew while the season was in full swing. A deeper sort of restfulness takes over; his attention turns more and more inward; he muses over the season that is past, and he sees how relative pleasure is. But he doesn't spend all his time reminiscing. In fact, new interests arise. He reads more, gives more of his time to thinking about problems to which he'd previously given little attention. New insights come to light. Interests become purer, more broadly human. He becomes interested in the people around him. In the bustle of the season they remained almost invisible. In a way he'd never experienced before, he sees the nobility of simple lives. If he is lucky enough not to be completely alone, then at the close of the season he is with his wife, who shares his life, and he begins to open up new conversations, to take a new interest in his partner's life.

"And, undistracted by the buzz of the full season, he comes to a deeper insight, a more intense approach to things. If friends and children come to visit only infrequently, even that is a different experience of loneliness than it once was. The person who at first denounced the deadness of these days slowly begins to take a completely new pleasure in this experience. In fact, he may talk about it too much; he prizes the 'afterseason' as the best of all possible times; he goes a bit too far and does not see with complete clarity how life was before."[2]

This piece by a well-known Dutch psychiatrist, who wrote it whan he himself stood at the threshold of the second half of life, is full of affecting images. And yet we do not entirely recognize in these images the elderly as we know them. In the first place, the picture it paints of the life of the elderly indicates that it was written before World War II. (Prosperity and increased ability to travel make the existence of elderly people much less isolated than is assumed here.) Moreover, the picture seems rather false. Positive aspects of old age are made too lovely, and, although the negative side is certainly indicated, it does not really seem to be experienced. Here I think we run into what Rümke himself appreciated when he wrote that this era of life cannot be fully understood, because the full meaning of a stage of life only becomes clear when it is actually lived through. Rümke, as a man in his middle years, is in the eyes of old people an outsider, and the kinds of images outsiders develop about older people become quite clear in this piece. It strikes a note of pity, conveys the notion that they no longer really belong, that they have in actuality already said their good-byes, and that they—despite all the serenity and deepening that are often present—have been shunted off to a siding after all.

In his inauguration speech upon assuming his professorship in Utrecht in 1933, Rümke explored more deeply the "deepening and serenity" to which people can come by means of analytic psychotherapy. In that speech he did not talk about aging people in so many words, but note his closing lines: "So analysis can help us to work through the whole problem of boundary situations, and to free the great problems of death and pain, conflict and guilt, from their childish forms, so that the matured spirit is placed at the absolute boundaries of human existence, and can, through accepting them and working them through, reach the highest pinnacle of development." We can hardly help placing that picture of the person made mature by analysis and the picture of the elderly person side by side: the elderly person, who through a confrontation with the fact of the finitude of his own life must show how "mature" he really is. (Munnichs, about whom we shall have more to say later, points out the fact of this confrontation.) Thus we see that this image of old age is a bit too blandly pretty. We have some difficulty recognizing in it the old people whom we know.

We must conclude that the aged in our society labor under the burden of a picture which we, and most particularly they, recognize as inadequate. Rümke makes it doubly so—and he represents, I think, much of current opinion. On the one hand, the old person is the one left behind after the season ends, who has been sidetracked, who no longer belongs; and on the other hand he is the person confronted with finitude who on that account reaches "the highest pinnacle of human development," or who at least *can* reach it. A man known by his wisdom, one might say.

It seems quite clear that Rümke's observation that as an outsider one cannot really write well about the elderly is absolutely right. But that has—and we must not forget it—particular consequences for old people in our society.

We have already mentioned the alienation between generations and the accompanying loneliness of older people. I have the impression that we are dealing here with a basic "given" that we shall come up against more than once in what follows.

These prefatory and orienting comments about the place of old people in our society are confirmed by the results of several small experiments conducted in various places. People have been asked to give, spontaneously, their first associations to the word *old*. It appeared that the associations were two-sided. On the one hand, they were negative. To the word *old* were associated words and ideas such as sick, weak, old-fashioned, grubby, uncertain, no longer able to follow a conversation. But on the other hand they were positive; people associated with *old* the words wise, sensible, experienced, peaceful, serene. These associations clearly indicate the kinds of images that exist in connection with the elderly. One must consider in this connection that such pictures are built not so much on the basis of empirical, objective observations as on the impressions that "outsiders" have of old people. Such impressions exist not only on the basis of observation but also on the basis of projections, which is to say that they are based on certain feelings. These results point us in the direction of the alienation and loneliness of the old in our society. The same applies to the observation made by Simone de Beauvoir in her book on old age.[3] She writes that one does not discover oneself to be old; it is revealed to one by others. It is the people who stand up to give us a seat on the bus, or the doctors who label our rheumatic pains as the common ailments of old age, who let us know that we are old. This too contributes to the alienation and loneliness of old people which we have already mentioned.

In my opinion it is these same experiences that we have to thank for the fact that we know comparatively little about old people. There is proportionately little research about them, and that only in the past few years. Most of what we know—and this, too, is curious—comes from medical science: people chatter easily about hardening of the arteries, memory loss, senile decay, and the like. In recent years sociologists and clinical psychologists have given much attention to older people, but their research has obviously encountered difficulty in reaching the wider public. It is clear that our images of old people hinder us. I would add that the observations we ourselves all make in the circle of family and acquaintances, where we regularly come in contact with our parents and members of their generation, do not induce us to form new images of becoming or being old. We all know a good number of old people who are very vital, who make long trips, who are interested in all kinds of things, who follow their hobbies, who even take on a number of functions in society; but our image of the older person remains largely untouched by all that. It is as if they—as suggested by the associations given earlier—must live up to certain expectations. Negative expectations concerning weakness, sickness, insecurity, and thus expectations of a person who can't get along without our help: but at the same time positive expectations about wisdom and inner peace, and thus of a person who can be an ideal and example for us.

What we are proposing, then, is that developing an image of the elderly cannot be separated from the fact that we hold on to certain feelings about them. They awaken such feelings in us, so to speak. On that basis I want to probe more deeply.

1. Many researchers point to the fact that the confrontation between young and old can evoke certain anxieties in the young. They see in older people, as it were, a part of their own future, and are afraid of becoming feeble and dependent. When one speaks with older people who are still in good health, the same anxiety seems to be present in them, as well.

2. In the same way, contact with older people awakens for many a kind of longing for more peace and wisdom. In the press and restlessness of their lives they hope to arrive at that point in the course of time; old people represent for them a portion of that future. In his study entitled *Religion in the Light of Psychology*, my former teacher Professor H. T. de Graaf wrote about old age, "The religion of this stage of life has an eye for the dream-situation of life; life becomes smaller and less meaningful. The majesty of what is eternal is more deeply felt, as over against the defectiveness and finitude of human beings. Sometimes there appears a pure serenity, as in the case of Jozef Israels, who said of the benefits he had received, 'I can't help that.' "[4]

3. Feelings in connection with the elderly may also lie at a deeper level. Older people are often unconsciously identified by young people with their parents. In that case, feelings arising out of the oedipus complex are going to play a role. Simone de Beauvoir offers many examples of cultures within which hostile feelings toward the elderly play a great part, while at the same time there is a remarkable need to experience them as somehow sacred. Somehow they apparently come close to the position of being a "holy secret."

Another inclination which is probably also connected with oedipal feelings is the tendency to pretend that the elderly no longer have any interest in, or thoughts about, sexuality. In a manner of speaking, discussing their sexuality is not allowed; it is suppressed, and if signs of it do show, words such as "crazy" or "dirty" are often used. That there could be a new and deeper form of the erotic—a possibility for which there is some clear evidence in our society—seldom is discussed. What is curious is that Simone de Beauvoir, who keeps an open mind about the sexuality of older folk, refers to this kind of eroticism almost not at all; to judge from her attitude she is also under the taboo of oedipal feelings.

The fact that such feelings—and the images that go with them—determine relationships with the elderly in our society is open to little doubt. Broadly seen, there exists an ambivalence of positive and negative feelings, with this dominant thought running through them: these are people who have had their time. Exactly here do we see the deepest roots of the alienation and loneliness of old people.

There exists in our time an obvious striving to come to more objective knowledge about, and deeper insight into, older people. This is especially true for physicians, psychologists, and social workers. But the images remain stubborn. The new science of gerontology is obviously blossoming greatly, but has difficulty in reaching the wider public with its publications. Gerontologists have already developed a number of important ideas. I think, for example, of the theories of Munnichs, who argues that on the basis of a confrontation with finitude the aging person comes to a disengagement, a cutting loose, after which there comes, if all goes well, a renewed engagement, but at a distance. Another important theory is that of the developmental psychologist Erik H. Erikson, who says that the task of the person in this last phase of life is to gain a certain sense of integrity, in the face of the despair and disgust which sometimes rear their ugly heads as we complete life's course. These theories will bear our closer examination.

2

Shifting Pastoral Patterns

One can call this book a pastoral-psychological study. It is a study written on the basis of pastoral-psychological research, and for those (though not for them alone) who have a pastoral relationship with older people. And so a brief chapter to orient the reader to developments in our contemporary society, especially with an eye to work with the elderly, will be useful.

I have a conviction that in our time a new outlook on pastoral work is gradually developing. In my book *Profiel van een Bedelaar (Profile of a Beggar: Being a Pastor in a Changing Society)* I discussed this change. I want to begin this study by saying that this development is neither accidental nor arbitrary; it is inseparable from deep, thoroughgoing changes in society. One can say that the pastor stands at the intersection of three lines. The first line is the institutional church, to which the pastor is more or less tightly tied. The second line represents human beings with whom and for whom the pastor undertakes ministry. Finally, the third line is the gospel (or theology), from which the pastor's calling, and hence a part of the pastor's identity, is drawn. These three "lines" and their intersection lie, as it were, in the broad territory of society, and all three, each in its own particular way, are interwoven with that society. The consequences are plain: whenever the society changes, that change sets in motion changes in all three lines. The church is going to function differently; human beings discover new thoughts and feelings in themselves; and we discover new aspects of the gospel. In what follows I want to try to bring a bit of clarity out of the fogginess that has prevailed so far.

We have to begin with the fact that we are emerging from a society that was marked by a number of clear characteristics. It was agrarian, craft-oriented, closed, and static, and could be seen and comprehended as a whole. It was a society of rank and station into which one was born and from which one could seldom break out. Although this condition prevailed more in Europe than in the New World, it was more true in America than many Americans would like to believe. The town or village was the clearest example. Such a community possessed several identifying marks; it held the individual to certain clear prescriptions for behavior. One was born to a particular rank or station, and by that fact alone one was bound by severe prescriptions for one's behavior, down to the very clothes one was expected to wear. The rules were especially strict about marriage.

Second, human life in that society was regulated by set "rites of passage" at such times as birth, puberty, marriage, and death. For the individual these rites had real meaning, because they gave each person a particular identity in the community.

Third, the life of the society was based on a "holy mystery." In using this term I am following Erik Erikson, who has tried at several places in his work to give his viewpoint on religion. He talks about the holy mystery of the "goodness" of life, that conquers death, sickness, and bad harvests. This mystery takes on a particularized existence in the divinity worshiped by the society. It is important to note that this divinity is always the "God of our fathers." That is to say, the connection with our forebears, our ancestors, always plays a large part. In his pioneering studies of totem religions, the French sociologist Durkheim indicated that religion is essential for the unity and inner power of a tribe; it is the great integrative factor in the society. We see this thesis proved in our own society. In religion—and later in the institutional church—the individual is connected to the community with and through his forebears. One develops "basic trust" in the "holy mystery" of the all-conquering goodness of life. As my former teacher, Dr. H. T. de Graaf, said, "He finds a place in the inexhaustible connections of life." In every society, religion and church serve both as guarantor and trainer in the structures, rites of passage, and holy mysteries of the society.

In this society the pastor may be variously seen as religiously privileged, as servant of the church, and thus as an "officeholder"; in any of these cases, the pastor has a clear mandate and authority: to define the society and its members in terms of the underlying mystery of the community. In sociological terms, the pastor is the representative of the social gatekeeping functions, but in such a way that he points beyond the immediate dimensions to those of transcendent mystery.

Traces of such communities are still to be found in our Western society; they are particularly still visible in the life of the church.

Yet it is clear that this society itself, with its identifying cultural patterns, is disappearing. In the Netherlands, since the end of World War II, a process of urbanization and industrialization has so altered society that the world we used to know is now preserved only in a few "reservations." Similar changes, some more sharply noticeable, some less so, have taken place in almost every Western nation in the past thirty-five years.

The new, emerging society has its own identifying marks. It is urbanized; it is functional (in the sense that people are connected with one another by means of their functions in the community); it is nontransparent, open, and dynamic. It knows no rank or station, and the most obvious form in which it appears is the metropolis.[1]

This urban, functional society displays some specific tendencies, too. We can see in it a development toward attacking old structures. People want to be free and to make decisions about their own existence. Rules imposed from above are discussed and, where possible, laid aside. In the area of marriage all kinds of experiments with new possibilities are taking place. Reactions of a conservative sort to these developments are also visible, but they seem to be developing in a fascistic direction, and have a kind of convulsive character to them. Another tendency is that rites of passage, so centrally important in an agrarian society, are more and more disappearing from present cultural patterns. There exist needs to "celebrate" birth, death, marriage, and puberty through some sort of rite or ritual, but such celebrations are becoming more and more a matter of personal choice and preference. They are no longer the possession of the society as a whole, and the society no longer takes part in the life of an individual through them. To put it another way, exactly at the point where individuals could at one time experience their place in the community—could, as it were, discover their identity—they now experience themselves made separate and their identities made vague. And as far as the holy mystery of the goodness of life is concerned, which we once encountered in religion and the church, it is now the subject of intense discussion; no longer is it to be taken for granted. People live with the idea that they must wrest the good life from the universe by their achievements. No one gets much closer to belief in a fundamental goodness of life than a stoic, negative agnosticism. Still others find any mystery of the goodness of life in solidarity with other people in suffering and struggling together, and no longer in any divine order of creation and re-creation.

Through this whole process we see the church shoved aside from a central place in society to somewhere near the margins. It has no clear, obvious function in an urban society, and seems to many no more than a relic of days gone by. This is even true where the church is looked upon with awe and wonder by large groups on account of the past and her part in it. In just a few places we see in and around the church the rise of new meeting places, where people meet in order to discover and clarify their religious experiences. In such religious experiences, God and our ancestors, who once occupied such a central place, are now the subject of search and discussion.

Because of all this we also see the role of the pastor gradually changing in character. If, as a representative of the church, he once was a man with sacred authority, now he appears more as one who accompanies people on their way to faith; not so much one who practices a divine calling by means of Word and Sacrament, but more one who has been initiated, a fellow human being who can help make certain things possible for us in our relationship to the "mystery": to use an American word, an *enabler*.

This means that all kinds of things are changing in the relationship between human beings and the church. First of all, there is still a large number of people who live according to the old patterns; they still find their identities in the old structures and rites of passage. Their ties to their forebears are still central for them; they experience those ties as ties between themselves here on earth and the Church Triumphant in heaven. For them, the task of the church in the world is still the worship of God's mystery, which conquers death, illness, and poor harvests, and which was revealed fully in the appearance of God's Son Jesus Christ. They read the gospel as the story, the message, of this strong God, Creator and Re-creator, even when such a way of reading the gospel finds hardly a single echo in our technological society—a society which puts far more emphasis on the role of the human race as creator.

Second, there is obviously a group which feels itself tied to the church as it developed historically, but which at the same time is open to the renewals necessary in our own day. Borrowing from the terminology of the Second Vatican Council, they speak of a necessary and possible "aggiornamento," an updating of the church; they want to rebuild the church so as to meet the needs of modern society. They want to use the church as a place of opportunity for the formation of modern believers, a meeting place for today's people who find themselves on the road toward (and with) the gospel, a place to celebrate the holy moments of existence.

Finally, there is visible in the society a movement of people who are obviously heading for new experiments to make the church and the gospel functional in a new way altogether. I think, for example, of ecumenical student communities, of South American liberation theology, of the pastoral work of hospital and prison chaplains, and of all kinds of new religious communities.

We have already said that the pastor is carried along with all these changes. It is expected of him that he will react to them creatively. That isn't easy. His mission and authority are less clear. He is more—as we said above—an accompanist: one who clarifies, unlocks possibilities, an enabler. He carries the expectation that his work will have an inalienable focus of its own, that through his words the gospel, Christ, and the church can be encompassed. But the places where his work borders on social work or psychotherapy or social action don't have perfectly clear boundaries. Among other things, we need in these times a bit of theological articulation; we need to emphasize that the task of the church is to bring together and hold together people who want to live as did Jesus Christ, and that the pastor, as a representative of Christ, as a symbol of the solidarity of these people in Christ, is to help people realize that goal. Jesus Christ is for us the man who, living in full connection both with humanity and with God, has caused a fellowship to spring up, a fellowship which amidst the sorrows of this world and the struggles for the quality of human existence lives on the basis of hope.

In this particular study our aim is fixed on the ministry among older people. This kind of pastoral work has two principal aspects. By virtue of such work, the pastor deals with people who for the most part grew up in the "old church"; he must understand them and support them in the midst of all the problems which arise out of the changes that have taken place. Yet these are also in a sense postwar people; in a way of speaking they are the sacrifices of present-day society. The rites of passage which played such a central part in their lives have now failed them. Their sense of their identity is seriously under attack; they miss the affirmation of a surrounding community. Thus the isolation of growing older strikes them perhaps even more deeply. If, with Erikson, we note that they must fight a battle for integrity, then we are forced to propose that any assumed trust in the goodness of an existence grounded in God's mystery will become the subject of doubt and discussion.

So we stand before a number of searching questions. Can modern pastoral work contribute anything to the solution of these problems, and, if so, how? What specific problems must be addressed? These are questions to which I shall return at the end of this book.

3

Some Important Viewpoints and Theories

One could say that the problem of the old among us was discovered after World War II, in about 1950 or so. At that time, people began realizing that in contemporary society, because of better medical care, we were going to have to deal with a larger number of old people. This called forth several questions. First, How shall we provide all these old people with appropriate housing? Second, Do we have satisfactory knowledge about the illnesses of old age, so that we can provide adequate medical and nursing care?

So we must notice that the old person is going to draw our attention in a particular way. People saw the old as those who belonged to a fast-growing group of people who needed help and had special needs for acceptable housing. Initially, there were two groups who responded to this perception. First, the physicians: they quickly brought into existence a scientific gerontology and geriatrics and built a cadre of trained nurses and other carers through the sponsorship of courses in these fields. Second, the church:

everywhere across the country it took initiative to develop housing for the aged.[1]

After about ten years, around 1960, there developed a reaction to this. People then began to wonder if the image they had of old people was really correct and if shutting them away in some kind of "home" was really a good solution. A third authority came into the picture: social work. New questions arose, and a new kind of research sprang into existence alongside medical research. The image of helpless, sickly old age changed into the image of an old person who will and must protect his/her independence, who should not live isolated from others, who needs to be connected to others as long as possible. In place of housing there developed service centers for the elderly, and public work with them. As a new group alongside the doctors, the pastors, and the social workers, psychologists started to become interested in the problems of the aged. In various ways, older people have become the object of psychological research. The psychologists' judgments are still rather fresh and provisional, and even somewhat biased, but something new has clearly been set in motion.

So we can say that our knowledge about aging people is growing, but that it is still one-sided and incomplete. The bias and incompleteness often spring from the need to "deal with" aging people as well as possible. We are busy trying to make up for that.

But there is a difficulty: there are conflicts in psychology over questions of method. How can this science, still very young, attain its objectives? I must devote some space to this problem, since it has meaning for a study of aging people.

One can, broadly speaking, distinguish between several schools of psychology, perhaps better called tendencies. The contrasts between Europe and America, and between psychology and psychoanalysis, are both important for us.

First, as to the contrasts between Europe and America. It is clear that there is no absolute contrast here; particularly in recent years has European psychology, in many areas, come under the strong influence of America. But the difference in directions remains noticeable to the close observer. One can get a good insight into this difference by looking at the book *Perspektiven der Persönlichkeitstheorie (Perspectives on Personality Theory)*, a book which emerged from a recent international symposium.[2] I think this is an important book which has not received the attention it deserves.

Let me try to sketch in broad strokes my own understanding of the contrast. The "view of man" in European science and thought is generally based, for the most part, on the romanticism of the nineteenth century. Using the word *man* means, in the preference of most Europeans, referring to a being that one can see as a whole person, something unique, and basically a mystery. One's purpose must be to understand, to comprehend, this being. And so in European psychology the influence of such thinkers as Dilthey and Spranger is still felt. We therefore want to understand, to get a whole picture of, young people in puberty and adolescence, as well as aged people. When we use the word *understand*, we mean that we want to enter into them, feel their feelings along with them, understand why they are as they are and think as they think. We aim ourselves at their personhood, at "the whole person." In America, and to a large extent in England, it is not romanticism but pragmatism that is influential in the view of human nature: one wants to do something, to accomplish something with people. Factory workers or students are not there to be understood, but primarily to be helped (made) to work better, to learn better. If we are to achieve this goal with them we must know a great deal about them. That comes about through the use of the most objective methods at our disposal to establish their intelligence, discover their skills, or get to know something of their character. The object of psychology is not the whole person, but rather human behavior, that aspect of humanity that we can pursue objectively, and from which we can draw valid, general, statistically reliable conclusions. So-called behaviorism, the psychological school in which this tendency is most clearly embodied, is a typical American phenomenon, although in European psychology the need to be as objective as possible is presently gaining the upper hand. Psychology wants to be just as objective, as exact, as the natural sciences, so that its researches can yield generally valid results.

What does this imply for the psychology of old people?

Two things, I think. There exist in our society two needs in relation to aging people. At the outset, we want to know more about them so as to be able to provide them with what they need: housing, medical care, provision for their social needs. Thus we need (the American theme) objective research; and we can say that such research is taking place, though still in a limited way. But in the second place we also want to understand older people better, to see them as people with their own possibilities, tasks, and limits, in order to have a better relationship with them. In European psychology, or in psychology with European roots (such as that of Erik Erikson, a psychoanalyst who lives in America but has his roots in Freud), we find attempts in this second direction clearly present. In the work of the most important Dutch gerontologist, Munnichs, we find both strains coming together.

The second contrast is the one between psychology and psychoanalysis. This is a contrast that has permeated developments in psychology over the last several decades, and is noticeable in the psychology of aging. We can consider the following. In the psychology of the human life cycle, to which an ever larger number of psychological publications is dedicated, old age is seen as a phase in the life cycle. That is, old age is a part of the life cycle in which human beings must go through certain experiences, complete certain tasks, undergo certain frustrations. In this phase each person scores certain victories and suffers some defeats. One of the tasks of the psychology of aging, then, is to follow carefully these experiences which are specific to aging, to trace them carefully and make them the subject of research. But two very different methods can be used.

First, the methods of objective psychology are used in research on aging. The important data for such studies are to be observed, recorded, and arranged. This is clear in such a study as the one done by Charlotte Bühler, an impressive study of the whole human life cycle.[3] Her data are taken specifically from the accomplishments of people; she starts with a view of the human being as the "animal that *does* things," a being that is concerned with performance, accomplishment.

Psychoanalysis stands in sharp contrast to this kind of objective psychology of old age. It also sees old age as a particular phase in the human life cycle, but comes at it from a different vantage point.

For Freud, the human life cycle is the way by which a person moves from a diffuse, uncoordinated, childish sexuality to fully developed adult sexuality, which is called "genital"; along that way, different phases can be distinguished. Erikson stands in the Freudian line, so far as his view of the life cycle is concerned, but formulates his view of human nature somewhat differently. He shows us how a person develops through various phases, each of which involves certain possibilities and certain tasks, from a childish ego to an adult ego. I want to show in this book how important this psychoanalytic research is for our understanding of aging. But I must add that for the ordinary psychologist who works with objective methods all this is not objectively verifiable, and therefore in his eyes is all rather arbitrary. We must return to this problem presently.

But first we must now ask, What do we need for a psychology of aging that these two directions can provide for us?

The answer is in some ways similar to the answer we gave to a like question a few pages back. We are in need of a better understanding of aging as a phase in the human life cycle. The psychoanalytic direction can open our eyes to the conflicts and tasks that the aging person meets in this phase of life. At the same time, we want to know more about aged people, and so we want to undergird our understanding with the results of empirical research. Here again, the work of Munnichs provides us with an example of a successful attempt to combine both approaches. But I must add that in terms both of understanding and of factual knowledge considerable need for closer examination exists. Such a concept as Erikson's "ego integrity" demands deeper reflection; so do such problems as the relation of older people to a concept of the hereafter, or the erotic life of the aged, or their relation to their own earlier life, and particularly to their own parents. These issues are all well known, but have scarcely been researched at all. Real psychological research, including pastoral-psychological research, into the lives of those who are growing older, has yet to begin.

In this chapter, which is designed to orient the reader to psychological research about older people, I shall mention a few important theories.

First, the work of Charlotte Bühler. She develops her theories in a study dating from 1932 on the human life cycle as a psychological problem. (A second edition of this book, actually not as good as the first, appeared in 1958.) Bühler considers the human life cycle in general, and in particular the phase of aging. Several of her observations are worth noting:

1. If one attempts to represent the life cycle of a person by means of a graph or curve, one discovers that the "biological

curve" (on which one could represent body and birth, blooming and wilting) is quite different from the curve representing the vicissitudes of the spirit. The biological curve runs ahead of the psychological, as it were. Athletes age faster than intellectuals.

2. The psychological curve, as Bühler sees it, is especially determined by achievements. In the area of human achievements we see several particulars: (a) that after a period of experimentation people come, when they are about thirty, to something more specific, so that by means of the tentative (in, for example, the choice of a career) we come to the definite and specific; (b) that when we are about forty we undergo a "change in dominant themes," in which the need to grow gives way to a feeling that one must fulfill one's duties; (c) that as we age we curtail the number of areas in which we operate, while at the same time there arises a need to come to some kind of balance with regard to our lives. From this quick summary we see that Bühler represents the objective side of psychology. For her it is more important to develop knowledge than understanding. The more subjective and emotional aspects of human existence have little interest for her, although one must say that now and then she puts us in touch with interesting problems. For example, she draws a distinction between transcendent and immanent life cycles (Søren Kierkegaard is an example of the former); and she introduces such concepts as destiny and fulfillment to the idea of the life cycle. But in general the passages in which she deals with these themes suffer from a treatment which is—at least for my taste—not deep enough.

3. The phase of aging is thus essentially for Bühler a phase of limitation. One is going to set boundaries for oneself. The older person is at work on a kind of cutting himself off.

In the second edition of her book Bühler offers a number of quotations from the German statesman and scholar

Wilhelm von Humboldt (1767-1835), written in the last twenty years of his life; from these selections it is clear that von Humboldt was curtailing his activities while he wrote about his own coming death, his hope for possible new life, while looking back over his life and taking leave of it. The interesting thing in all this is that again and again he steps into his experience as a preparation for stepping into activity; first he expresses feelings and opinions, and then decisions follow after a while. For Bühler, this last period of life is a time when one is busy with one's own departure and future.

At points such as these the limitations of objective psychology become noticeable. Bühler brings together much important material, and her classification of phases provides an orderly arrangement, but her image of human beings, controlled as it is by notions of accomplishment, by seeing humans largely in terms of *homo faber* ("man the maker"), misses a deeper and more insightful understanding. She simply does not touch such questions as: How does a person achieve a balance? How does a person experience the completion of his life? or How does a person consider the past and the future?

A second theorist is Munnichs, whom we have already named a few times. Munnichs is one of the most important Dutch writers in the field of the psychology of aging; in his book, *Ouderdom en Eindigheid (Old Age and Finitude)*, written in 1964, he developed his theories on the basis of a widespread study of a large number of aged people.[4] The book was followed by several articles which did not modify the basic arguments of the book.

His principal thought is that the aging person, by means of experiences which affirm the finiteness of existence, comes to a point where he "disengages" from life, and then comes to a renewed engagement, but this time at a greater distance. Munnichs depends in part on the theory developed by the Americans Cumming and Henry in their

1961 publication, *Growing Old*.[5] That book sparked a lively discussion in America about the fundamental characteristics of aging. One saw that older people became less active, and one asked: "Is that desirable?"

A wide range of research projects was undertaken. One such project was aimed at social and psychological disengagement and the relationship between the two. The research showed that psychological disengagement precedes social disengagement, an observation which recalls Bühler's remarks about experience preceding activity. Second, there was research about the relationship between disengagement and a concept of "life-satisfaction." Is the older person really content with this letting go of all kinds of activity? It appeared that there was no simple answer to this question; the aging person clearly wants, on the one hand, to remain active and to retain a sense of self-respect, but on the other hand longs for a more peaceful existence. In the third place it became clear that personality differences played a large part: the need for engagement or disengagement is dependent on the personality of the aging person, his life history, and his life-style. All this proceeded on the assumption that the disengagement is fundamentally connected with the preparation for sickness and death which is necessary for the aging person. From a social viewpoint the disengagement is both desirable and useful. But at this point the theory of Cumming and Henry misses a number of other themes which to some critics are important: the self-awareness of aging people, the fact that reengagement is often not noticed, that a number of aging people (many politicians, for example) never disengage at all, and the twin facts of better health and a longer old age.

To this American discussion Munnichs brought a new hypothesis. The confrontation of the older person with finiteness (which is somewhat different from death) is, as he sees it, a decisive element. That confrontation leads to a social and psychological disengagement, to be sure, but through that disengagement to a new, psychologically somewhat different, engagement. I think we may say that Munnichs gives a more European tint to things. He attempts to push more deeply into the experiencing of the aging person, and then to connect that with the concepts of engagement and disengagement. He says that older people struggle with the problem of having to accept the finiteness of their existence, and that if they succeed in that, they are able to "let go," but through that letting go they are able to "pick things up" again, but now in a freer way. And so for the older person the problem of the acceptance of their finitude is the important problem, and we do not succeed in solving this problem without some difficulty. It comes in phases; that is, there are critical moments in aging, and we shall return to that theme later.

We get, I think, a clearer understanding of what Munnichs is about when we make a comparison with the grief process; there, too, one encounters the idea of letting go in phases. We can probably also relate it to the problem of identity: our society has no role for old people to play, and by that fact it attacks their sense of identity. Can that possibly be without effect on the way in which they work out the problems of this last phase of life?

These are merely a few marginal notes, but it is clear that Munnichs brings several important ideas into view with his approach.

The third theory is that of Erikson, who develops original ideas about the phase of old age in his overall conception of the life cycle. Erikson is a psychoanalyst of the Freudian school. In his thirties he emigrated from Europe to America, where he developed into one of the leading figures in psychoanalysis. In his book *Identity and the Life Cycle* he develops his theory of life stages and devotes several pages to the problem of aging.[6] Three aspects are important for him:

1. He sees life as a continuum of eight phases following one after the other. In each phase people live, so to speak, between two poles, and the task is to make the positive pole one's own, a task in which one never altogether succeeds. Thus, in the first phase (corresponding to Freud's "oral" phase), the child makes its way between the poles of "basic trust" and "basic mistrust." The task of this first phase succeeds only if one enters the next phase with a fairly complete measure of trust.

2. The eighth and last phase occurs in old age. In this phase, as in the others, we must complete a specific task; here the two "poles" are "ego integrity" and "despair and disgust."

3. Erikson sees human life as always embedded in and correlated with social relationships, which play in each phase of the life cycle a role of their own.

Let us take a closer look at these three points.

First, in order to get a good grip on the nature of the last phase it is a good idea to sketch in brief the entire scheme of eight phases. They are connected with one another and presuppose one another throughout the life cycle.

The first corresponds, as stated, with the oral phase, and spans approximately the first nine months of life: its "poles," as we have seen, are *basic trust* and *basic mistrust*. In this phase the relationship with mother plays a central part.

The second phase goes from the ninth month to about three years of age, and corresponds roughly to the Freudian "anal" phase. Its poles are, on the one hand, *autonomy*, and, on the other, *shame and doubt*. Here again the relationship with the mother is of central importance.

The third phase is the well-known oedipal phase of Freud, and is marked by *initiative* on the one hand and *guilt feelings* on the other. In this phase the relationship between fathers and sons, or mothers and daughters, is in the foreground.

The fourth phase, from the end of the oedipal phase at about seven years of age to the beginning of puberty at about thirteen, called in Freudian theory the latency phase, has as its important polarities *industry* and *inferiority*. At this point it is the relationship with the school which is influential in development.

Puberty and adolescence form the next phase, marked by a sense of *identity* on the one end and *identity confusion* on the other. Here the relationship to society as a whole is essential.

Following this phase comes that of young adulthood (20-25), where the poles are *intimacy* and *isolation*. Here a significant other person is formative.

The next-to-last phase is adulthood, lasting till one is about sixty. Here *generativity*—being productive in one's relationship with the next generation—and *stagnation* or limitation in this productivity are the two poles. In this phase the family and the work environment are the most important relationships.

Finally comes an eighth phase: old age, lasting from age sixty until death. As we have already said, the two poles are *ego integrity* and *despair or disgust*. What is curious here is that Erikson does not speak about social relationships in connection with this phase. In the course of this book we shall see from time to time how important the lack of a relationship with the society around him is for the aging person. Erikson, if true, gives us to understand that he sees the aging person as experiencing himself in the succession of generations, as a link in the chain between ancestors and descendants, a context that reaches beyond death. (He also makes it clear that he thinks of himself as one who experiences the feelings of older people.)

The second aspect of Erikson's work that we should discuss is the task the aging person must fulfill in this last phase. Erikson refers to integrity, but it is not so easy to make clear just what he means by this. Doubtless he has something exact in mind, but it is something that cannot be made clear. One may wonder if he is not creating too pretty a picture here, if perhaps he is seeing something as ideal for the aging person which he himself has not experienced because he is still young. In the first chapter we saw something quite similar with certain parts of the work of Rümke.

What does Erikson say about integrity?

I shall give some indication of what he says in his book. In old age, if all goes well, the fruit of the previous seven stages ripens. When one describes this fruit with the word *integrity*, there is a certainty of order and sense to it. One can surrender leadership, accept one's own unique life cycle along with the people who were important in it (including particularly one's own parents), accept responsibility for one's own life, develop a feeling of comradeship with similar people in earlier times, defend the value of one's own life-style, and develop a feeling of being connected with those who have gone before. Here Erikson uses the word *wisdom* and speaks of a self whose identity is confirmed in "what of me lives on." We may say by this that he implies death is accepted positively. The opposite pole of this integrity is despair or disgust: a person cannot accept his lot or his death; he wants to live life over or try other ways of living it, but time is too short.

We note, as the third aspect of our comment on Erikson, the embeddedness of human existence in social relationships. How is this related to the aging person, as Erikson sees it? We have already seen that Erikson is less clear about this than he is in his definitions of the other phases.

In Erikson's thought patterns, social relationships have for the individual a double meaning. They give us, as it were, a niche, a place where we fit, where we have a foothold: family of origin, school, present family, work. Second, they provide a positive foundation for basic trust, which every person must have in order to live; they offer a place where we feel secure. On the basis of these two points there arises for the aging person a problem: aging people no longer have a niche, and they miss a meaningful "place to be," where the society around them gives them security. One must ask whether the context of succeeding generations, which Erikson introduces, and through which we experience a part of our identity, is for many too little understood or experienced, especially if they have no children. It is just here that I get the feeling that Erikson's whole schema is a bit artificial, a bit too pretty. On the other hand, I must say that, in my understanding, Erikson, with his introduction of this context for the aging person, has brought up an important if not essential aspect of human living, one which has received far too little attention in the present view of humankind, and which requires deeper consideration.

Finally, I indicate one other important point. In the course of life there is also—as psychoanalysis clearly shows us—a kind of "duet" between psychological and bodily development: talking and running abilities and sexual maturation all play an essential role in the various phases. All things—the body, the psyche, the social context—are entwined with one another in human development throughout the life cycle.

Is that also true of aging?

By and large, Erikson does not say much about the relationships to the body. Still, there are clear developments with reference to the body which we should note: sexual interest dwindles, memory becomes limited, mobility grows less. Is that matched, as bodily processes are matched in the first years of life, by a psychological, and possibly a social, change? The correlations with social development are perhaps not so clearly demonstrable as they are in childhood, where just the ability to walk brings with it a revolutionary change in social relationships. But they are certainly present; retiring is clearly connected with the deterioration of physical abilities. As for the correlations with psychological change, we have no clear picture of them, but we must consider them probable. Researchers indicate that there are within the phase of aging sub-phases to be noticed. I think it likely that within them connections with physical change will be noticeable. I shall return to that in a more detailed way later. Here, I think, is a fruitful area for research.

To close out this chapter, a few more remarks. The following insights strike me as central:

—growing older involves a restriction of activity (Bühler)
—growing older demands a "coming clean" about the finitude of life, and, on that basis, coming to a disengagement followed by a renewed but more detached engagement (Munnichs)
—growing older demands that ego integrity win out (Erikson).

In the balance of this book we shall return to these insights via various paths; we shall then have the opportunity, as well, to make corrections and amplifications.

Second, I note that in the foregoing material we have also made the acquaintance of several special problems in the lives of old people, which will still require our attention in what follows: preoccupation with the past, being hampered by unfinished business out of the past, redressing the balance of life, dying, one's relationship with one's own body, the appearance of phases within the aging process, and probably still more.

What we may certainly say is that aging in the human life cycle is more than just a process of undoing things or perhaps a period when things are calm. It is a time of quite fundamental tasks and developments. Two aspects of this spring immediately to our attention. Human beings must learn to let go; perhaps we can speak of a grief process through which one rounds off one's life. This is a task which can obviously go wrong, and we may ask, How does that happen? Perhaps through "unfinished business."

Dante once compared aging with striking one's sails as one enters a safe harbor. This image calls still another image to mind: hoisting one's sails in youth, when the boat is about to leave the harbor and make for the open sea. Both the hoisting and the striking of sails must be done with care and cooperation, and in carefully timed stages. Aging, like being young, is a task and an art.

4

Older People in Modern Society

One of the fundamental thoughts in Erikson's work is that the identity of a person—and therefore of older people—is in part determined by the society in which the person lives, and specifically by the expectations society has of him and the tasks which it, on that basis, assigns to him. What would that mean for older people in present-day society? What are the most important hallmarks of our society in this connection?

First, a few facts.

The picture that our society gives in relation to older people is a picture of polar opposites. On the one hand, society shuffles people off to retirement at age sixty-five without making any distinctions between persons; it does so hurriedly and without so much as an "excuse me." When I think of the term Erikson introduces in connection with adolescence, the word *moratorium,* I am inclined to call this process "expulsion"; there is no moratorium; one is simply kicked out. On the other hand, this same society then surrounds the aging person with all kinds of care such as pension plans, social security, special prices for senior citizens, and retirement and nursing homes. We might note in passing that the care is strongly bureaucratized.

It seems to me that there is a great chance, psychologically speaking, that aging people will be isolated and estranged.

What leaps to mind immediately is what Margaret Mead was talking about when she wrote in her 1970 book, *Culture and Commitment*, about what she called a "prefigurative culture."[1] As Mead saw it, one encounters a prefigurative culture in a society where the older people no longer teach the children, but just the reverse; the children are ahead of the older people, and the older ones must learn from the younger. For example, a society like our own, in which the development of knowledge and technical skills is so rapid, recognizes that many older people are no longer "with it," and will have to learn many things from their children.

In a prefigurative culture all the emphasis is on being young and learning. Such situations are known in societies built up out of immigrants, such as the United States of America and Israel. People consider the ideal time of life in such societies to be the period from eighteen to thirty; older people are quickly thought of as old, and much money is devoted to education. It is clear that Western European society resembles these "immigrant" societies in many respects. Education department budgets are growing to gigantic proportions. A graduate engineer, according to many people, is no longer up to date after reaching the age of thirty-five, and in a large company these days he is likely to be located in a spot where his experience, rather than his knowledge, is important.

It simply seems incontrovertible to me that we need to be talking about isolation and estrangement in such a society.

A third fact is that the image which one often has of more primitive cultures usually includes the idea that old people, because of their wisdom, occupy a central place in them. One thinks immediately of the Old Testament and particularly of the Book of Proverbs, or of the Council of Elders (like a Senate) among some primitive groups. This image is not entirely inaccurate, but it must be seen as somewhat relative. Simone de Beauvoir never tires of repeating and repeating the names of peoples who in the past (and to some extent in the present) neglected and even mistreated older people in a horrible way. Research has established that the more idealized picture of older people is valid for the so-called upper crust; in these same societies poor old people had a very hard lot and were sometimes even put to death. As a young man I often had occasion to notice how farm workers, after fifty years of faithful service, were thrown aside by their rich employers without the slightest pension.

One can also ask to what extent this negative feeling toward older people is informed by an unconscious wish on the part of younger men to shove older ones aside and take their place, an unconscious wish that forms a part of that whole collection of feelings which Freud called the Oedipus complex. Oedipus was the prince in Greek legend who killed his father and married his mother. The fact that the Ten Commandments so specifically spell out the command to "honor thy father and thy mother" may very well be connected with the fact that such honor is not equally self-evident to everyone, and may give some people quite a lot of difficulty.

What really is the identity of older people in a modern society, and what is it in a primitive society?

A. In modern society it can be said that the knowledge which older people possess quickly becomes obsolete, and that the experience of older people, so often highly spoken of, is just a relative concept. The work that must be done is becoming in modern society increasingly complicated, one of the results being that the desire for early retirement is increasing in many lines of work.

It must be said, too, that in our society the identity which a person possesses is given almost exclusively by the work he does. You are someone through your work and for as long as you work. This means therefore that older people in our society have almost no identity; that is, society expects nothing of them and gives them no work to do. Of adolescents the same thing naturally holds true; they, too, complete no tasks in the concrete sense of the word, and the society lays on them no concrete responsibilities. They have received a moratorium from the world around them. But there is a difference: adolescents do have a task visible just as soon as they look at the place they expect to have in the future in society. That in turn involves a set of expectations. Adolescents' identity comes from the fact that they are to prepare themselves for their place in society and their identity in it. But it is precisely that element which is lacking in the relationship between the community and the aging person. The aging person receives from the community, by means of a pension, a certain space; but for what purpose? For an *un*social task, actually, or at least for a task that has no relevance in the framework of modern society, namely to "work on himself" with an eye toward his eventual end. As Munnichs argued, the aging person must try to come to terms with the fact that his existence will have an end.

Whether the aging person accepts that task or not, and how the aging person tries to accomplish it, is not of the slightest interest to the community. The community has no images about that task; on the contrary, the community finds it anxiety-provoking. Is not this one of the underlying causes of the alienation between society and old people?

B. In a more primitive society identity problems lie elsewhere, for the most part. Older people are those with the most experience, whether one is talking about work or about child rearing, about human beings or about society. Much of that experience is stored up in all kinds of proverbs or sayings, and by means of such sayings old people take part in the formations of opinions and decisions. They can also participate longer in the work process; when their powers diminish, they can still do all kinds of things on a farm or in a trade, so long as they are set to less demanding jobs. The consequence is that there is no period of life when one retires, and, for the most part, no such thing as rules and regulations for retirement. Thus there is much less talk of alienation, such as we hear in our own modern society; in fact, in a primitive society a person still has, by means of the tasks he fulfills and the expectations people have of him, a certain identity. He *is* somebody.

There is still another aspect to the question of identity in older people. In a more primitive society—and this time I am thinking not only of a small tribe but also of a village or even of a smaller city—older people often have a highly specific function. In the Old Testament we read of the (usually old) men who "sit in the gate." In the Netherlands, in the little harbor towns by the Zuider Zee, one finds along the harbor walls so-called "liars' benches." There one could see—and sometimes one can see them still—old men from the town, telling stories of days gone by to anyone who will listen. In America, one can see the same phenomenon in county seat towns, where instead of sitting along the wall of a harbor, the old men sit on benches on the courthouse square. In either case, the stories told often resemble the heroic myths told in primitive tribes. Among those listening nearby are always young men. The stories are of great significance for them; they arouse and enlarge in them a sense of connectedness with the town or the city. The stories are about their past and their heroes, and create in them an experience of connectedness just as happens when the members of a tribe hear stories about *their* past and *their* heroes. Older people thus become the mediators of tradition for posterity, creating a relationship with the past, and thereby with the city itself.

By means of these stories there develops a kind of "group strength." In our own Dutch Hindelopen or in Mount Sterling, Illinois, or in a New Guinea tribe (different as all these are from each other), the people have frequent times in their history when it was a struggle to stay alive. In the stories and in the connectedness between older and younger people were themes such as courage and trust. So older people in such smaller communities have a function: through them the communities live with, and out of, their past. Through the myths and stories one finds in one's forebears a bit of security, a belief. It is partly for this reason that the Old Testament contains such an ample account of the past, or that the names of the martyrs are recounted in the old liturgies of the Roman Catholic Church. It is for the same reason that so much teaching of history was and is a set of stories about heroes of the past and their victories.

And so in primitive societies older people have a particular task, and must live up to certain expectations. From that they gain an identity. Perhaps it is a rather vague identity, difficult to describe in specific terms. But it is real nonetheless; you can still find it in the structures of our family life; the portrait galleries of old English castles witness to it.

Such an identity becomes much more vague in modern society. Here the principal accent is no longer laid on the relationship with the past and its heroes, but on the relationship with the future. We have to give thought to education of people for new perspectives, and to whether our knowledge is keeping pace. The myths told in a primitive society are unreal to us, and the stories heard from the "liars' bench" are rather ridiculous. Old people have no contribution to make to our generation, and so they have no identity. We have all kinds of duties to them, of course, and we acquit ourselves as well as we can, but just the same we do it in a bureaucratic, impersonal manner. In the Fir Forest of Breda, where I lived until recently, there are many benches with old men sitting on them; one can see the same groups of old men on the benches on the town square in Holton, Kansas. In Holland, they arrived on well-kept bicycles; in America, in a well-kept pickup truck, perhaps with a van top built into the back. In Florida, they drive in such vans along the interstate highway, perhaps with a bumper sticker reading: "No cares—no worries—no work—no money." They are well dressed. But they are by themselves; one sees no younger people with them. Young men, if there are any, are roaring past on cycles or in sports cars.

A few general remarks as we near the end of this chapter. In modern society there appear to be three major periods in a human life cycle.

The first is the period which comes in the middle of life, the time when we are participating in the work force and/or rearing families. Family and work—Freud's "love and work"—are the principal elements of life in this period. What Erikson means by his term "generativity" comes to life in this period.

The second important period is that of preparation. It includes the various phases in which the human being, from the time of being a babe at the breast, is preparing for adulthood by means of all kinds of growing and working on himself. From the time of cuddling up in mother's lap (where we develop a basis for living through the establishment of Erikson's basic trust) through adolescence and after (where we develop an identity and try to develop the capacity for intimacy) we are actually in a process of "growing into" a larger society, into which we eventually step by means of certain "rites of passage." Society provides us with a moratorium, a period when we can experiment without committing ourselves to a particular life or career. Along with that, these "rites of passage" can be compared with the initiation ceremonies which give structure to the entry of young men into adulthood. The possibilities of the body play a great part in these years of preparation; through a combination of play and formal schooling one learns to discover and to use his or her body. This element of putting one's own body at one's disposal is of fundamental importance for the building of a sense of identity.

The third period is the one which begins more or less abruptly when we retire. It means a sharp break with a living pattern built, up to this point, on generativity. After preparation for and realization of the "purpose of life," there follows a period of letting go, tearing down, and moving toward one's end. Up to now, the study of this last period has been largely devoted to its psychological side; the problems especially looked at have been disengagement and renewed engagement, confrontation with finitude, and preoccupation with the past.

But it seems quite clear to me that, just as in youth, the body plays an important role here. The possibilities of the body, which in youth continually expand, now continually shrink. The question can arise whether there are not, as it were, problems in the other direction. We could put the expanding physical possibilities of youth over against the diminishing physical possibilities of old age. Are living without demands or responsibilities, and the development of hobbies, perhaps to be compared with the play of young people, and is perhaps the expulsion of retirement comparable to the initiation of youth? If that is the case, is it not possible that, just as a young person is given a moratorium (in part for the purpose of practice) in order to prepare for adulthood, the aging person should be given a period of transition in order to prepare for retirement?

In fact, we can take the comparison a step further and ask if there may not be particular phases in this period, parallel to the phases in youth. Could not paying attention to the possibilities of the body be of help here? We are not far enough along to say more about that at this moment; I shall return to it in the last chapters of this book.

5

Examples of Aging People

Before going further, we shall examine in this chapter some examples of aging persons. The intention is to test and perhaps to sharpen our sensitivity to what affects older people. In the first half of the chapter there is a newspaper report with a letter attached to it, in which a retired man pours out his heart to a friend. I shall ask you, before you read further, to formulate for yourself what you learn about the possibilities and perspectives of aging people from such a "human document." Then I shall make my own observations about it, so that you can compare your thoughts with mine. In the second half of the chapter we shall follow the same procedure, using four short sketches of aging people and their contact with a pastoral worker.

Here, then, is a newspaper report and a letter related to it. It is about a lawyer who is retiring. The report appeared in a local newspaper—shall we say Medford? Springfield? Centerville?—under the heading "Local News."

Last Wednesday a very heavily attended reception was held in the law offices of Smith, Brown, and Jones on the occasion of the departure of Mr. John Smith, who is retiring from the active practice of law on his sixty-eighth birthday. Mr. Smith enjoys a reputation not only in our own city but in the wider world. He was for many years a member of the city council and held the chair of many local committees. He was a member of several national committees of the Lutheran Church. Many people attended the reception. In addition to the mayor, representatives of a large number of organizations brought greetings. They commended his vitality and effectiveness, which still seem undiminished, his lively and alert personality, and his warm humanity, which have made him many friends in every circle of the city. Many speakers wished him a period of well earned relaxation after a busy career loaded with work, but also expressed the hope that, given his vitality and many interests, he would find a way to continue making contributions to community groups and organizations.

A few days after the reception, this same Mr. Smith wrote a letter to a long-time friend in response to the friend's letter about his retirement.

Dear Jim,

Thanks a lot for your letter. It's been a long time since we've seen each other, but a letter like yours reminds me of the many conversations about many subjects that we've had over the years and prompts me to set down some thoughts, not only for you but also for myself.

Yes, it was a tremendous reception. Many people were there and there was a lovely tone to the party. All kinds of people had something to say. And I got very clearly the feeling of a more or less definite end of something. At the office there are a couple of cases I'm following and I'm still sitting on a few boards. But when you get to this point, you call it a day, and what you "call a day" is perhaps everything you've called your life. In any case, this retirement has certainly started me thinking.

The first thing that hits me is that thoughts and feelings arise in you which you can't share with anyone. I don't know if there's a taboo on talking about them—maybe that's part of it anyhow. It's a bit strange, but it goes deeper than that; it's like something you're ashamed of, a kind of weakness that you're not supposed to tolerate in yourself, but there it is, it's part of you, and it belongs to everything you do from now on. And I have the feeling that it's difficult to talk about it because if you do you arouse all kinds of anxiety in people, particularly younger people, to say nothing of yourself. But I think I can deal with these things with you, specifically with you. A clear feeling that I have is one of being loose, of being free. And I must say that's not a good feeling.

Maybe it's that way for a lot of people—I hear retired people say that now they can get at things they haven't been able to do up till now—but my feeling, despite the fact that I still have plenty to do, is that I'm being thrown into some kind of vacuum. There is a psychiatrist who wrote that people who retire ought to keep up their daily rhythm after they retire, getting up at the usual time, going out the door at a fixed time even if to spend the morning walking in an open field, coming home at the time they always did. I've always found that idea a bit overdone, and I still do, but now that I face that same situation myself I begin to think that it has some merit. What comes to me when I consider being loose or free is something that runs deeper, a feeling of being thrown back upon my own resources. I don't belong any more; in fact, it's more than that; it's that now I belong to the group labeled as not belonging, a group whose members have to solve, piece by piece, the problem which that raises for them. It's very much like the *apartheid* of South Africa; you're cut off by a kind of "color bar" from those who make up the community.

Another idea that has come to me makes that feeling of standing alone even stronger. In one of the speeches at the reception somebody said that he hoped that I'd stay active, because "You're only as old as you feel," and so if you keep active you'll get old more slowly—that, at least, was the idea. Well, there is something in me that says "yes" to that, and at the same time there is something that says that you're off and running for something that you have to want and have to be able to do. There is something in me that says a man must dare to be old, be able to be old, if he lives long enough to have the opportunity. Quitting, retiring: that means crossing a boundary; it's a real rite of passage, and in the new territory there's a road ahead of you that you must travel. Deep inside, I feel that that's not easy. I can still do a lot, my body is of course not what it once was, but it still obeys me pretty well; I'm still interested in all kinds of things. Yes, I know, I'm in danger of overestimating myself. But you can't escape that. It has something to do with calling a halt to your career, the end of your prestige in society, your life among other men.

And that brings me to the other thought that has already come up at several points for me, and that's the thought of death. All these end-points point irrevocably toward death. I have to say that whole days go by when I don't think about that, but there are periods when I think of it every day in one form or another. A couple of years ago I was even especially depressed about it, and now and then a kind of depressive "fit" comes to the surface. Death has always played a part in the background of my existence; I often had to go to burials or cremations, but I found that a trial, and sometimes I could hardly say a word. The odd thing is that that's all better now—I have the feeling that I can think more realistically about death as the end of my life. This end has its place, and in one way or another your life makes you grow toward it, I think. But I must say again that sometimes, in those depressive spells, I think with sadness and reluctance that my life may be over within a few years, and people will be standing by my grave. But what I think is, that there's such a thing as growth even in this area, and a person ought to develop the art of living in growing older, too, and that means growing through this part of life. That means you know about your depressive spells, but you also know that there's no solution for them. You have to be a little passive, and with a little acceptance, you'll get over it in a while.

Another thing. Thoughts about work play a big part in what you go through in these months. I'm still tied down to some parts of my work, which satisfies me somewhat. I take as much pleasure in it now as I ever did, and I hope that will last a long time. What you certainly recognize, however, is that you can't do as much as you once could, and some things lose their attractiveness. (Not much trouble handing those over to someone else!) As far as feelings are concerned, there's less need to be in the limelight or have successes: things that play quite a part in the practice of law. It's as if the grip which our so-called performance-oriented society had on you relaxes. And in connection with work there arises a need for, and an enjoyment of, freedom. It's as if you experience your work more as a hobby.

And finally there are certain things that you could not get at earlier, which now take on a real value for you: contacts with your wife, your children, your grandchildren, your friends, and even with art and nature. Not so much because they connect you with the past (I don't live in the past very much) but because of the warmth, the light they bring.

Thanks for listening.

Cordially your friend,
Jack

Let me now propose that you, the reader, write down five points which you have noticed and which you feel are hallmarks of growing older. Below I shall give my own observations. Comparing the two can help us sharpen our sensitivities. It is possible that you will have noticed different things, or more things, than I did. Thinking about that or talking it over with somebody can get us farther along.

My own observations are as follows:

1. I am struck by the opposition between what is said in the community (in the newspaper and at the reception) and what this lawyer himself feels. The newspaper mentions his vitality, his activity, the fact that he is an extravert, his involvement in the community. His own feelings point in another direction: he talks especially about departure; he makes a rather introverted impression (I notice how busy he is with his own inner feelings), now and then he is depressed; his work is secondary. This man must feel a bit alienated from those who are close to him.

2. In fact, he is quite busy with his own inner thoughts, and with himself. I assume that Munnichs would say he does it in a meaningful way. That, according to Munnichs, is our task in these years. It demands a good deal of introspection, which this lawyer seems to possess in rather full measure. And here there arises a question, Is every aging person quite as conscious of this problem as our man seems to be? Don't we have to say that many people are not bright enough or articulate enough to think about themselves in these terms and to express themselves so well? And then, Aren't there many people who are afraid of looking inside themselves this much and who thus block themselves from this kind of necessary inner development?

3. One feels from this letter how important it is to have someone with whom to talk about these problems. The writer says in fact that he is grateful to his friend for listening. If he had not had the chance to share his problems

with someone else, he really would have been stuck in a lonely place. To be able to talk about oneself and one's internal problems—with another person or perhaps in a group set up for just that purpose—is an important need of older people.

4. In an interview in a church news magazine, Professor H. R. Wijngaarden calls this period an "adventure." But when one reads this letter one gets the impression that this word is not exaggerated. From what the writer says, it seems that he is caught up in a demanding process; a lot is happening inside him and he has a lot to work out. His body is not what it was (think for a moment about the changes in sexuality alone); his mental powers seem to be slipping (people complain about their memory loss and how it creates a new kind of dependence); he has had to give up a great deal (his work, his traveling, his little pleasures); limitations (death) have come within his vision; he makes new discoveries with his children, his grandchildren, and in nature. Externally, a variety of things can happen, as we know, to an older person: he may have to move; he gets sick, or those close to him do; people he cares about die; he has to cope with divorce in the families of his children; and we have not even mentioned the things he reads every day in the newspaper.

5. We also see in this letter that retirement brings with it certain problems. In this case, it really is an "expulsion," with no time to get ready for that, no period of adjustment to it. All kinds of sources of strength, all kinds of things which provide inner strength and inner peace for people without their being aware of it, disappear without much preparation of any kind. The daily rhythm of work, as Rümke calls it, is gone. So is the completion of assigned tasks, the feeling of being needed (which is part of generativity), and a number of other things which signal a person's place in the community. Things do remain, of course: family, children,

and friends. But the writer is really talking about a vacuum; the overall sense is that he has been expelled.

6. What is striking, as the writer sees it, is that a period begins in which there is a clear facing of an end to existence. He writes as if he is on the verge of learning something. We see in the letter how this has to do with falling and learning to stand up all over again. It is clearly a process in which one struggles with letting go, and is therefore a grief process. One can ask whether there are separate phases to be distinguished in such a process. There probably are; other researchers have already written about that. One may well ask whether there is a kind of aggression at work here; and I believe that we must say that there is. To grow old often is to grumble.

7. What the writer of this letter says also arouses our interest in the area of death. For him, death has come within the realm of possibility. We cannot make out directly from the letter if this is more the case at one time than at another. Research suggests that there are in fact critical moments: for example, when one approaches the age of sixty-five. What is striking is that the relationship with death in aging persons changes its character; a certain familiarity begins to show itself.

8. He talks about his relationship to his work. It is still demanding, but not so much as it once was. He emphasizes the freedom he is now feeling, now that the community is no longer surrounding him with demands. There is a kind of playfulness (he mentions a hobby) which reminds one of younger years.

Now, here is a second letter to his friend, written a year later, which gives us some sense of what he is feeling after a year's interval. We can notice in this second letter that the writer has worked through his feelings of expulsion, but that the basics of the process announced, as it were, in the first letter, still lie ahead.

Dear Jim,

You ask how I'm doing now that I've been retired for a year. I don't really have a lot to offer. Things are going well, and I'm happy. My wife and I are both healthy. We're enjoying all kinds of things that we can do now that we're free: walking, bicycling, visiting our friends and our children, traveling, reading, watching a little TV now and then. I'm still doing a lot of things, including some work, but not too much, and really only the things I enjoy doing. The pressure of a profession and of needing to bring in money is off, and I feel that a relief.

What I notice is that the idea that now and then people need you for something or other (and that you have meaning for other people) is very important. In the background, or maybe in the underground, of my life there is, I think, a sort of void or a sorrow that I don't clearly feel, but I notice the remains of it in my reactions to people.

I also notice that sadness or problems among my children occupies more of my attention than it used to, and the burial or cremation of someone I know sets me to thinking more. You could say that I've become more vulnerable, but I rather think it's a process fulfilling itself in me, a kind of knowledge that life has changed and somehow that has to do with being retired, a kind of knowledge that this is the last phase of life.

The colors are lovely, and we—my wife and I— are enjoying them, but they are autumn colors. Now and then we say to each other that we are doing well with each other, but we don't know how long that will last. The odd thing is that we don't find that depressing. The depressed spells that I had right after I retired I haven't had for some months now. On the contrary, it excites us to live more positively, to take each day as it comes. I think that the whole thing is a process that's been going on for some time, and will keep going on. The trick will be not to resist, but to learn the language of this phase as well as possible.

It's pleasant to have contact with you now and then. Friendship is important.

Cordially,
Jack

Now we turn to sketches about four other people. I have borrowed them from the doctoral dissertation of P. Brouns, submitted to the theological faculty at Tilburg, and entitled "Reflections on Pastoral Work with Old People."[1] Brouns worked for some months at a service center for the elderly as a pastoral worker, along with a number of psychologists and social workers. In his essay he describes a number of old people with whom he had contact, and on the basis of his data I have assembled these sketches. I propose that once again you, the reader, should write down your observations about the most important elements of aging as they are revealed here, and then later compare your notes with mine, which follow the sketches.

Four Portraits

Mrs. Mott

Mrs. Mott is a seventy-five-year-old widow. Her husband died seventeen years ago. She still has six children: three "boys" and three "girls." (Two other children died shortly after birth.) Mrs. Mott comes to the service center regularly to get some exercise and to have her feet taken care of. The social worker helped her make application for a housing subsidy and get her telephone connected. She told him that she felt lonely. When he asked her if she would like a pastoral visit, she was quite agreeable. I visited her for the first time in September 1972. She impressed me as a pleasant old lady who cared for herself well; she was short and neatly dressed. Her house seemed clean and well tended. She rents out the upstairs to a nurse, but maintains no other contact with her. When I told her who I was, she received me in a friendly way. She said it was nice to know that someone was thinking about her.

The basic picture I got held up throughout my contacts with Mrs. Mott. She is a seventy-five-year-old widow who thinks about almost nothing but her children. In caring about their problems, which she has done all her life (two of them have gotten divorces), she has steadfastly remained on their side. Life seems heavy to her and affects her nerves. Sometimes she'd just as soon be dead.

As far as the outside world is concerned, Mrs. Mott gives the impression that it either seems threatening to her, or ought to be ready to take her orders. She is very critical of other people. For that reason, she is pretty much alone. A feeling of social helplessness seems to predominate in her.

Mrs. Best

Mrs. Best is fifty-eight and seriously ill. She is married and has two sons, twenty and eighteen. Her husband works in a large business. The visiting nurse asked Mrs. Best about the possibilities of a pastoral visit. She accepted the offer eagerly. She told me she is suffering from chronic kidney disease and that the doctor has told her she will probably never see sixty. For the most part she is lively, but now and then she suffers from depressive spells. Most of the time she stays in bed. When I visit, she sometimes gets up and sits in a chair. The family lives in a rather old house, simply furnished. Mrs. Best's bed stands in a corner in a downstairs room. She no longer goes upstairs. There are many plants and flowers in the house. Mrs. Best is not very big, and has gray hair; she looks older than she is.

The area in which the conversations with Mrs. Best take place is an open question. From the very beginning she puts her trust in the pastor. Outside of the family, the family doctor and the pastor are the people to whom she brings her problems and questions. There are few in her family or her husband's, and they all live far from the city. Moreover, few people ever come to visit. Relations in the family are good. Mrs. Best carries her pain in a dignified way. Despite the pain and the necessity of staying in bed she does her best to be a mother, wife, and homemaker for her family. After the talk about all kinds of daily events, other themes come in for repeated discussion: her illness, how she is experiencing it, thoughts about dying, working through the past, and how to care for her surroundings. Thoughts about death are not alien to her. She is tied to that. Dying itself, and the moment of death, arouse anxiety in her. The nearness of death gives her life a separate dimension. On the one hand she is trying as intensely as possible to live, but on the other hand she already feels herself partially gone. Acceptance alternates with protest: it could have been so nice, we could have done so well.

The past also comes repeatedly into the conversation.

Her childhood was hard. Mrs. Best herself thinks that is partly the cause of her illness. Still, she bears no hard feelings. Her first marriage was unfortunate. After the divorce there was a tug-of-war over the child born to that marriage. She was deeply offended by that. Later she married again and with her second husband's help got over it. Now, as she lies ill, she thinks back to that time a lot. She has a longing to clean things up with everyone before she dies. In her conversation about all of this Mrs. Best tries to discover the meaning of her life: why did all this happen and what have I done with it? The balance comes out positive. She is satisfied with the course of events and with her role in it; it has been good. She strongly believes that we do not have everything in our own hands; one must accept the inevitable. The mystery of "why" remains unsolved. The things from which she draws strength are her faith, her care and concern for her family and other people with whom she comes in contact. Her life has a faith dimension, although she is not a practicing Christian. We can say that the pastor, by listening, helps Mrs. Best get a clearer view of her life. The pastor himself had the impression that he could have done still more.

Mr. Berg

Mr. Berg is eighty-two, and has been a widower for fifteen years. Since his wife's death, he has lived with his only child Joe, a sixty-year-old man who lost his wife five years ago after a long illness. Throughout the time that Mr. Berg has lived with his son, he has done the cooking and the housekeeping. His daughter-in-law was always sick. Joe, disabled by a lung illness, has not worked for several years. At an appointment with the social worker, Mr. Berg put on a lot of pressure to be admitted to a retirement home. He had vague complaints about the situation at home and wanted out as soon as possible. The social worker asked me to look into Mr. Berg's complaint and, if possible, to help him; it probably would take a long time, for there was a considerable waiting list.

Mr. Berg lives in a simple house in a working-class neighborhood. He walks with a little difficulty, but seems younger than eighty-two. He always wears a work jacket. The house is well kept—all the work of Mr. Berg. He says that with the advancing years things seem to get more difficult. His comment about the difficulties comes across as realistic and without exaggeration. His son has a relationship with a divorced woman, who lives with one of her children, and every night the two sit drinking together. The son is a heavy drinker and uses his father like a drudge; he is supposed to take care of everything, and gets scolded if it doesn't please them. Now the woman moves in with them, and things quickly get worse; Mr. Berg goes into physical decline and would just as soon be dead. The relationships in the house are becoming tense.

From the welfare office comes the news, in connection with the pastoral visit, that Mr. Berg's request to be admitted to housing for the aged will be examined by someone from the office soon. This gives him a little hope, but it seems as if the case—despite the efforts of the pastoral worker to speed things up—is going to hang fire. Mr. Berg is obviously getting feebler; medicine from the doctor helps only a little. After five months, a visit from the welfare commission helps very little; Mr. Berg's name is on two housing lists, but is moving very slowly up those lists.

Meanwhile, his son dies, and Mr. Berg gets rid of the woman. Now he is alone in the house and it is not long after that that the doctor determines that he can no longer live alone, and orders an immediate admission to a nursing home.

Mr. Berg presents a picture of an isolated old man, who, in a difficult situation, longs for some peace and for more contact with other people. The longer he stays in his situation the less he can stand it, but admission to a nursing home raises all kinds of difficulties. Socially he lives (like many old people) in an isolated position, stuck in the house with few people if any in the community paying any attention to him. In the home situation he meets with little love or comfort. The pastor helps him with sympathy and with concrete mediation, but the man himself keeps sitting with his problem, coming up against the structures of the bureaucracy. For Mr. Berg there comes a moment when he finally asks what the sense of it all is. "Do I deserve this? I always did my best." It sounds like a complaint against life, a life which hits him harder and harder. Death seems to him a welcome liberation. Fortunately, the admission to the nursing home finally comes through, late as it may be, and life has something to offer Mr. Berg once again.

Mrs. Rock

Mrs. Rock is a seventy-four-year-old widow who spent her life among truck drivers and campers. Her life history is full of moves. Her first husband died during World War II, and she remarried in 1957. Since then she has lived, as she puts it, "in a middle-class home." Her only child, Rose, was born in her first marriage; she was murdered in 1946. Mrs. Rock took her daughter's three children under her wing, but the Division of Family Services took them away from her. The death of her daughter caused her a great deal of grief. She also finds it hard to swallow the fact that she has no idea what has become of her grandchildren. She has no family for all practical purposes. She has almost no contact with her family, which is spread all over the country, because she is essentially illiterate.

The social worker who came to talk with her about her diet mentioned to her the possibility of a pastoral visit, which she accepted happily. I visited her once every three weeks for about ten months.

Mrs. Rock is a little lady with a wrinkled face, a bit overweight. She is somewhat deaf, wears big earrings, and always wears a flowered apron over her slacks. Her house is old; the whole neighborhood is up for renewal. The walls are hung with copper and brass baubles; the tables are loaded with various shiny things and pieces of porcelain. She has a dog, a parrot, and a couple of tame blackbirds. The whole thing appears shabby, but clean and well-kept.

Her health is reasonably good. She has very high blood pressure, which often makes her dizzy. She is also short of breath, which keeps her from walking very far. She cannot always accomplish what she sets out for herself, which annoys her. Every day she does at least one thing: clean a room, do the laundry. She is almost never sick ("Living outside has made me tough"). Every once in a while things get too much for her, and a longing to be on the road again overtakes her.

She wants to shift for herself and maintain her independence. She lives on welfare and is "getting rich on sleep." She is painfully honest, has firm convictions, is grateful to those who are kind to her, but will have nothing to do with anyone who does her a disservice. She enjoys chatting with people on the street, but, with a few exceptions, does not really know any of them well.

She is very grateful to the pastor for his visit. She tells him many kinds of things about her earlier life: her daughter, her own childhood when, because her family was rich only in children but poor in everything else, she had to beg in the streets and was beaten if she brought home too little. Her father spent a year and a half in prison for abusing her. And she talks about the time after the death of her daughter; she wandered through the countryside for six months with the three grandchildren and then had to give them up to Family Services, after which she never saw them again. The pastor does his best, in consultation with her, to track down the grandchildren, which finally succeeds and leads to a reunion. This in turn leads to a lasting contact, by means of which they go back and forth visiting each other. Mrs. Rock feels as though she once again has a family, which means a great deal to her.

In her own neighborhood she also has contact with children, who come to watch television at her house, and who, with the help of the pastor, are teaching her to read. The pastor has done a great many things for her: he has broken through her social isolation, has listened to her, and has actually been of concrete service to her. By his intervention she has come in closer touch with her past and is becoming a fuller person.

What strikes us in these four portraits?

1. My first thought is about the alienation one can sense between these people and the surrounding community. As seen in these sketches, aging people form a separate group with separate problems and special difficulties, which the community apparently barely notices, and to which it assigns little importance.

2. These are people who are preoccupied with themselves. They have problems with their children, with housing, and possibly with their work. But their chief problem is themselves. In all the sketches is also hidden the problem of dying or at least of growing old. Thus we see how aging includes a particular developmental task.

3. It also seems that being able to talk about their problems is important for these people. The pastor finds a part of his role here. From American pastoral care literature

we know the image of the pastor as one who helps people grow toward maturity. We see something of that here, too. I do not mean to say that the role of the pastor ends here. But as one who has a knowledge of the deeper truths of human existence, he can help people grow toward maturity by making underlying problems emerge into the open so that they can be talked about. I have discussed the various aspects of the role of the pastor more extensively in my book, *Profiel van een Bedelaar*.[2]

4. It is also striking how much is happening in these lives. In fact, their lives are in many respects adventurous. Life for them is neither dull nor empty. Growing older does not mean having no more experiences—that is the least of what it means—it is full of a number of important tasks.

5. In all four cases, even with the "industrious" Mrs. Rock, there is an obvious facing in the direction of an end to life. This element is not to be thought of as outside their existence. It gives their lives a particular coloration, and even a particular content.

6. In all four cases, death is visible as an element. Sometimes an audible companion, sometimes a silent one, death shows itself most clearly in the problems of the body. Sometimes death is used as a kind of shield: against oneself as in the case of Mrs. Mott, or against others, as in the case of Mr. Berg. Death can be tied to thoughts of vengeance or to thoughts of liberation. Here we are also up against the problem of suicide, quite common among the aging. From the vignettes we can see that thoughts of suicide can more easily arise for these people than for young people. One may well wonder if there is not an implicit but unconscious longing for death in these people. What we can see just as well in the vignettes is that genuine anxiety about death is not openly discussed, although there is certainly anxiety about dying present, as we can see in the case of Mrs. Best.

7. A relationship to work is present but not emphasized. It is largely work in the form of actively keeping house, as in

the case of Mr. Berg. Here we should notice that there is a different relationship to work for women than for men, when the work is housekeeping. Working at making a home is less of a burden imposed from the outside. It can be a form of self-expression, and sometimes take on the flavor of a hobby. One sometimes gets the impression that there is not much difference between artists and housewives in their relation to their work. In the case of Mrs. Rock work has a special meaning: for her it is a burden which she lays upon herself. She *must* be neat; it is a kind of defense. Her earlier life plays a decisive part here.

8. For that matter, this is a factor which is obviously of significance for understanding aging people. The portraits of Mrs. Best and Mrs. Rock indicate this clearly. One cannot lump all old peole together. All of them must fulfill certain developmental tasks (such as coming to terms with the end of life), but they will do so in an individual manner derived from their own life cycle.

9. In the portraits there appears a need to come to a kind of evaluation of one's life. Mrs. Best and Mrs. Rock and, to some extent, Mr. Berg want to come to a sort of balance. This has much to do with trying to come to that sense of ego integrity which Erik Erikson describes. People have a need to value their lives in a positive way and to develop a sense of gratitude rather than a sense of despair.

10. What we also see is the social isolation of these older people. Not one of the four has obvious contacts outside of the immediate family. Family and children must then provide the confirmation which all people need. Without their children these people would become more or less helpless quite quickly. Mmes. Mott and Rock and Mr. Berg are all examples of that.

11. On the other hand, children sometimes seem to deal badly with their parents. Both Mrs. Mott and Mrs. Rock are examples of this. It is a quite frequent occurrence. Simone de Beauvoir devotes several pages to it, and every pastor in

his life has met poignant examples of it. The parent-child relationship is on both sides loaded with ambivalent feelings of love and hate. Freud's Oedipus complex is a real thing.

12. In the world of the elderly we run up against the problem of structures. Mr. Berg almost becomes a sacrificial lamb for the bureaucracy. Rendering help to old people is to a large extent an organizational matter. The administrators of retirement residences and those who run social service agencies play a big role in this world, with a large chance for impersonal contacts. Stories about this are legion. So much so that we must take warning against being drawn into stereotyped caricatures about such people. There are after all many good ones.

13. *Housing* is an important matter in almost every case. There are two reasons for its importance: first, it has to do with the almost complete lack of contact with other people and the associated problem of isolation; second, there is the problem of being in a condition to care for the house or the apartment where one lives. The view usually taken of this problem at the moment is that the aged should maintain their independence as long as possible and must not be placed in retirement homes too early. This certainly seems right, but I surmise that the problem of isolation is not always taken into consideration.

14. What we also notice in these four cases is that there is little talk about faith, in the traditional sense. The image that one occasionally encounters about older people, that they are (or should be) more "faithful" than others, does not seem to hold up. This does not exclude the possibility that in this phase of life certain faith perspectives are visible—or can be, or should be—just as they are in any phase of life.

On the basis of these portraits one can certainly say that old people are no more "churchy" than others; we see no evidence of church interest in the vignettes. Of course, one cannot draw conclusions from four sketches, but the observation is worth making.

15. The general impression from these four vignettes is that a threatening isolation quickly leads to helplessness and that old people have but few possibilities for helping themselves. In their powerlessness they get into emergency situations or are driven into repressed rage.

Here we must also observe that these four cases are not representative of all or even of a majority of old people. They are only a small selection, drawn from one man's attempts to help people. Not all old people get into a situation in which they need help. But we may draw the conclusion that when certain essential conditions are missing for old people, they quickly get into the kinds of situations described above.

6

The World as the Aging Person Experiences It

The title of this chapter requires clarification. What we want to indicate in this chapter is best compared with what Carl Rogers calls in his books "frame of reference." As he points out, he tries in his counseling conversations to remain within the "frame of reference" of his clients. They express certain thoughts and feelings and these, taken together, make up the "frame of reference," the world that they at this moment are experiencing. How does Rogers know this world? By listening as carefully *as possible* to them, and, more than that, by *being* with them as empathically *as possible,* by thinking and feeling with them as much as possible. Thus he is able to be "with the other" as intelligently and sensitively *as possible,* so as to "live with" their thoughts, feelings, problems, motivations, so as to see the world through their eyes, and to enter into their inner world as they experience it as a whole. Rogers does not try to describe or analyze the *behavior* of the other; his method is not objective. Instead, he tries, with his own feelings, to experience what the other person says or does.

As pastors we are interested in the experienced world of the aging person in just this way. We must step into their world, as it were, in order to work with them. In fact, I believe that this is valid for every helper as well as for the members of old people's families. It is not important what we *know* about them when we are in contact with them, but whether we can *experience* their thoughts and feelings with them, and thus whether we can help them, want to help them.

In this chapter I try to paint the world of the aging person and thus to make a contribution to better understanding. There is no easy way to do this. A combination of methods is advisable: description, entering in, clarification of structures, moving toward deeper understanding by recalling certain thoughts and feelings and connecting them with deeper motivations. I have to try a process of observation, empathic thinking, and empathic feeling.

What kind of material is at our disposal for this purpose?

Of course we can build a foundation out of all the research that has been done in the field of gerontology. And then there is a treasure of experience, of observations by pastors and other helpers, that can help us. Finally, there are the observations that I, as an aging man myself, have made, as well as the observations of my contemporaries. I think of Rümke's observation that one has to have experienced a life phase before one can adequately describe it. It is understandable that the book Stanley Hall wrote about old age after his own retirement is still quoted. I am of course conscious of the subjective element in all of that, but I hope that there will be enough objective elements in the picture I paint to guard against any accidents.

The Relationship to the Society

How do aging people experience their relationship to the society around them?

It has become apparent in previous chapters that as a group and as individuals there is mention of alienation and consequently isolation. This is not difficult to understand. We have a picture of the human life cycle: we classify both the biological and psychological "curves" in such a way that in the middle of the phase of adult life there is a plateau, a high point. This phase of greatest physical and mental ability is the most important period of our lives; we really live for it. The concept of *dismantling* undergirds both aspects of the human life cycle. Hence retirement, after this phase of adult life in which one takes full part in the life of the society, can be experienced as a kind of expulsion from the community. It is with this fact that the chance for isolation and alienation begins.

Let us also not forget that this is all complicated by certain emotions. Even older people know the uncertainties of ambivalence, which is the hallmark of so many human relationships: tenderness and intimacy on the one hand, and distance and aggression on the other. In their relationship with society there is the distance of the bureaucracy, impersonal and businesslike, on the one hand, and, on the other, the closeness of children and contemporaries. These are two poles which stand next to each other, over against each other, and cannot be reconciled. What adults have in their families and their work relationships, a daily connection between the two poles, is missing for the aged.

Let us look more closely at the problems that are involved here.

When we look closely at a somewhat more primitive society, we notice that there is much less talk of alienation. In villages, and specifically in farm families, one sees less of it. There is less emphasis on performance and production and more on experience. Older people can participate for a longer time. And when their abilities are no longer sufficient for hard work, there are corners where they can make themselves useful. Grandpa sharpens the knives, peels the apples, and feeds the animals. Is there a feeling of expulsion there, too? The opposite is true; there is a position, comparable to the moratorium of adolescence. The older person gets the possibility of growing into older life. In this society there is also more chance to have an identity. We have already seen an example of that in an earlier chapter. This applies not only to men; women, too, have an identity and a function. Grandmothers play an important role in family life. But we must also realize that this more primitive society is disappearing more and more, and with its disappearance come alienation and isolation.

In modern metropolitan life the chance of isolation and estrangement is much greater. This estrangement is accompanied, for old people, by a number of phenomena that we must discuss in order to get a good picture of their world of experience.

a. For people who retire, it usually happens that they gain a feeling of liberation. There is still a lot we want to do, one hears people say, but it is so nice that we no longer *have to* do it. It's clear that in present-day society work is primarily experienced as a series of obligations, which for aging people feels more and more like a burden; that certainly will lead to a feeling of freedom when one retires. People can return, as it were, to an earlier life pattern, the one experienced in adolescence before initiation into adulthood. People are heard to say that they can return to themselves and to the things on which they actually place importance. That is a return to the things which belong to their deepest identity.

b. But with the falling away of obligations comes also the falling away of that affirmation which people receive from their work. They no longer hear that people are satisfied with them; they no longer see that they have accomplished something. We lose the notion that is essential for a sense of "generativity," to use Erikson's term, namely, the sense that one is needed. People have a deep need to be needed. People often react to the loss of work with a depression. There are also well-known cases of people who soon after retirement, when the celebration of retirement is past, come down with a mysterious illness. The sickness is psychosomatic; one works off a kind of aggressiveness by means of it. Another possibility is that people respond by becoming helpless, unable to stand on their own two feet; this manifests itself in a need to be dependent, often on one's spouse.

c. One of the effects of retirement is that people are thrown back upon their own resources. This phenomenon is also to be compared with the period of adolescence, and, as in adolescence, there is a chance of identity diffusion. When work disappears, one can hear in the background questions like, "What is my place?" or "What is my job now?" or "What can I still do?" Behind such questions lie deeper questions: "What am I worth?" or "Who am I in my own eyes and in the eyes of others?" We do not see our roles clearly, and there comes the danger of playing fake roles. One thinks that one can still participate in politics; one thinks that one is not yet sexually "written off." In social situations one prides oneself on taking roles that one has previously taken.

d. There is another place where old age is like adolescence. Isolation and estrangement lead to the formation of groups. In work with the elderly one can see clubs rising out of the ground like mushrooms. Peer groups perform a particular function in puberty and adolescence. They give a sense of identity and provide participants with a sense of belonging, as well as a chance to "rap" with one another; through this conversation members can come to more clarity about themselves and a better grip on the problems of life to come. Senior citizens' clubs provide more than just a bit of amusement; they also give an opportunity for necessary conversation. Senior citizens' passes and sixty-five-plus tickets to things also have a contribution to make to a sense of identity. One knows oneself to be more than just an isolated person, but a member of an important group in society, as well. I expect that in the future this group will take various kinds of initiatives, and that action-oriented groups will form. (This expectation has already come true in the U.S.A. in such groups as the "Gray Panthers," *trs.*) With the strengthening of a concept of identity and the increase in their number will also come the feeling that one must grow into certain forms of responsibility. I do not believe that this will lead to older people capturing an organic place in our modern society. Our society will not permit that. They will remain, like migrant workers and children, a group on the outskirts.

To sum up, we may say that aging people in this relationship have to deal with a process in which they experience a certain amount of alienation which has to be worked through and integrated. It is comparable to a grief process; it demands that we let go of something to which we have an attachment. We shall see that old people have to undergo a similar process in other areas of life.

Relationships to Work

In the foregoing material we have already spoken about this relationship. Now we need to go into it more specifically and more deeply.

We begin with several observations. Old people often remain quite active in the area of their work. For doctors, artists, politicians, housewives, and farmers there is really no such thing as a pension or a retirement age, and it appears that they often keep working long after what is retirement age for other professions.

In growing old, people limit themselves. Charlotte Bühler has called the limitation of the dimensions of life the hallmark of the last phase of life. Scientists, for example, concentrate on a smaller number of research projects.

The stakes are often less intense for older people. It seems as though a certain emotional distance is built in. Munnichs speaks, as we have seen, of a renewed engagement in distance. The farmer leaves certain decisions up to his son; the creative artist loses some of her longing to renew herself; physicians look for a more quiet practice; and pastors take smaller congregations. This lowering of stakes becomes clearest in the phenomenon of hobbies. With a hobby it is not so much a matter of the result but of the pleasure one gets, of "doing it for the sake of doing it." Here there is clearly a parallel to youth; in youth one often plays for the sake of playing. Psychologically speaking, hobbies and games are not far from each other.

Giving up work has certain consequences. Here are a few: (a) with work, the tension over performance and results falls away; (b) away from work one is no longer tied to a "performance group" as one is in a factory or office; (c) one gets no affirmation from supervisors, and one can even get the feeling that one is no longer needed; (d) with the disappearance of work the structure of the day or of the week falls away. (Compare Rümke's advice to stick to one's schedule after retirement as much as possible.) This of course does not hold for the groups that we have mentioned above: doctors, artists, farmers, and housewives, who do not give up their work all at once.

Thus we see how the giving up of work has an interfering influence on the human ego. In reality it is a blow to one's self-confidence. As we have seen, affirmation, which is important to a man and which he gets largely from his work, disappears for the most part. Now one gets that from one's children, wife, and hobbies. The result is a certain loss of ego-vitality; men who once held positions of leadership in public life now fill their mornings with shopping for their wives, chatting over coffee with friends in a coffee shop or with their wives at home, discussing the recent rise of a few cents in the price of bread. This thinning out of possibilities can itself lead to a kind of identity diffusion; one gives up the identity of mayor or company manager and what does one get in its place?

Still more happens as a result of giving up work. The circle of people and problems in which one moves becomes smaller. The circle that one still has comes therefore to have unavoidably more meaning; children and friends come more within the daily round of things. But now that the sphere of interest becomes smaller and the reality of the world comes in from farther away (older people live more than they once did by the radio, television, newspaper, and stories told and retold), the reaction to this reality becomes more negative. Grumbling, particularly about politics, often gets the upper hand. In general, one can say that vitality is certainly still solidly present but that it is not, in a manner of speaking, stimulated or put to work; there is something there that one could well compare with freewheeling or coasting. Here, then, we encounter a particular aspect of the aging process: giving up work has a backlash on the ego and on family relationships. Here again we have to think in terms of a grief process.

Two more brief remarks. Women who lose their husbands lose both some of their identity and some of their work. They often say that they have the same problems we have discussed above: confirmation and regularity both disappear and the backlash from that is felt.

About the aging of people whose aging does not necesarily involve retirement—farmers, housewives, composers, painters, actors, politicians—we really know very little. Research seems to show that their health is better than that of their contemporaries. Goya and Rubinstein are examples of the fact that people of advanced age can still be quite capable of performance and that the idea of growing rigid is not always necessarily the case. One wonders whether the relationship such people have to their work is not influential here. For them, work is not necessarily something imposed from the outside or an obligation within a particular group; the accent lies more on a bit of self-fulfillment, where there is still room for development of one's own initiative. Could it be that living and working within the patterns of the third phase of life (which, according to Erikson, is the phase of initiative) keeps these people young? This, then, is in contrast to those who have worked primarily within the patterns of generativity and for whom the end of that phase is a confrontation with the end of life.

Relations to Others (Contemporaries)

Research into the way older people spend their time has shown that they invest much time and energy in their relationships with their contemporaries. Aside from their families they have little contact with people in other age groups.

What is the nature of this contact?

The accent lies on the things that people do together. Doing things in groups that are not too large, such as bicycling, swimming, playing cards, sitting and talking on a bench, is clearly a fitting form of contact. What we see is that the elderly are not drawn to each other on the basis of common convictions. They are not going to found a church or a political party: there is no political or religious vision peculiar to the aged. At best, they can come together for concrete purposes: action groups or "trade unions" of old people are thus easy to imagine.

I see in this phenomenon of the formation of groups among old people a counterpart of peer groups among adolescents. As we know, such peer groups in adolescence have a great role to play, and have a specific function:

to help in the formation and building up of identity. Clubs have a function for the elderly which runs in the same general direction: they offer a sense of identity. On the basis of a common destiny—being old—they provide regular contact and doing things together. They thus strengthen one's security as one wrestles with the problems of being old. Clubs offer, if I see it correctly, no contact on a deeper emotional level. It is thus not "friends" that one meets there, people with whom one is in the deepest sense familiar. It is not just older men but also older women who have such clubs; they obviously are also seeking this kind of contact.

We may say that the deeper contacts of old people are to be found in the circles of the family and a few old friends. Yet seldom are the aging genuinely intimate with their own children. As we have seen, Erikson suggests that the phase of intimacy comes just after adolescence. It is as though in the years of aging the line of development bends itself backward and the aging person enters a phase which is comparable with adolescence. We shall see that there are more phenomena which point to the idea that a development takes place in old age which in a reversed sense parallels the development in youth; it seems very much the case that aging people have to turn back toward their beginnings.

Relationships with Others (Middle-aged)

There is as yet little research in this area. The impression is that little contact exists between the elderly and middle-aged people. Apparently such contacts are not sought by either party. There are of course meetings, but these take place in the context of family gatherings. Even then there is a kind of distance between the middle-aged and the elderly, often a discomfort; seldom is there a genuinely intimate contact.

Even in more businesslike contacts—in the area of offering help, for example—elderly people seldom seem to be understood by the adults working in service agencies. For retirees, a visit to the office or the factory where they used to work often turns out to be disappointing. It seems as though one lives in two worlds; the isolation of which we have spoken makes itself felt and a feeling of aloneness comes to the surface.

What we may notice is the phenomenon of intimate contact that a younger person initiates with an older person. The younger seeks and finds an older person from whom one can ask advice and with whom one can express oneself as freely as necessary. I know examples of young women who had an older friend whom they had met more or less casually in the park and with whom they carried on serious conversations. About the reverse case, where older people sought out younger ones to ask advice, I have no examples; they seem less likely to me. One can wonder how it stands at such a point in the helping professions. Does a social worker or a pastor, who has much to do with old people in his work and who himself belongs to the middle-aged generation, have particular difficulties? Is the distance between them palpable? Experience teaches that the more the contact is professional, the less important is the age of the helper.

The decisive factor in the contact between older people and representatives of younger generations seems to me to be that they have no common interests and problems. They therefore easily pass each other like ships in the night.

A difficult problem can be to decide at what moment an aging person should lay aside membership in management. The difficulties are more of an emotional than a realistic nature. Realistically speaking, the contribution of a sixty-five or seventy-year-old is just as valuable as that of a younger person. But both the older person and the younger one have to consider the question whether it is not better to lay aside direction at a particular moment. I believe that we must recognize that the oedipal problem plays a part in this. Our society lays a particular role pattern upon us: older people form a group which at a particular time of life must step aside or be shoved aside. Younger people have guilt feelings in connection with this, and older ones are not always reasonable about it. We shall have to learn to come to realistic and open discussion.

Relations to Others (Young People)

What strikes us about this topic is that our society has a tendency to be led by certain images, such as:

—older people are good for children; they pamper their grandchildren. Or, older people often find children "too much"; they are too strict with them.

—older people no longer understand modern youth: their clothes, their ideas, are all too far from their own experience. Or, older people can often talk very well with modern young people; they experience in them something that they themselves were not able to do but would have liked to do.

—older people can become the confidants of young people; they can support them, understand them, give them advice. Or, older people can only make jokes about young people; they are awkward when in actual contact with them.

It is clear that in this territory we still know very little. If we want to speak with any certainty, more research will be necessary.

What we can say at the moment is that we encounter ambivalence in the attitudes of many older people toward younger ones. They feel drawn to them on the one hand and have a positive attitude toward them; sometimes it is as if there is a mutual recognition of oneself in the other, something that is connected with what we have already noticed, namely, that there are parallels to be seen in the lives of older people and youth. There is also in older people, especially in grandparents, a trace of generativity in their relationships with younger people; they are interested in them and in their future, they want to talk to them, pass something along to them. Several books have appeared in recent years consisting of letters from older people to their children or grandchildren. But there is the other side, as well: a certain feeling of negativity toward young people. It springs from a certain weakness of the ego; as old people they feel insecure, sometimes even anxious. Especially toward young teen-agers with all their vitality, their tendency toward violence, and their chaotic behavior. It is as though they feel they are encountering, especially in the big cities, an alien and threatening world.

Relationship to the Church

In this area, too, we still know little. We find a good insight into what research has turned up in America in the article by David O. Moberg, "Religiosity in Old Age," published in the collection, *Middle Age and Aging*. The impression that one gets from the available data is that among older people there is less "investment," and thus less participation in society or church attendance, than there is with younger people. But, the author suggests, this may also be connected with the fact that older people are less steady on their feet, or that in bad weather they must stay away more often.

In general it seems to be the case that the factors which earlier created a positive attitude toward the church are still present in old age. There is really no new motivation visible toward the church. Whatever people found in church in earlier years, they will value in the church now, as well. We shall give explicit attention to religious factors later; for the moment we shall simply point to the feeling of (religious) companionship that one finds in the church. The church is also an important factor as a part of the society; belonging to it and participating in its life provides a bit of identity and self-respect. Moreover, the church is, in the life of large groups, a weighty factor, because it plays a part in the social control of individual behavior. Finally, the church offers important help in education and in the making of moral choices. In the Netherlands, far more than in the United States, membership in a religious group plays a large part in the choice of schools, political parties, and sometimes even in one's career. This particularly Dutch phenomenon, called *verzuiling* (columnization), means that in our country the church has had a deep influence on the lives of millions of people. In general, people do not want to lose this as they age, and so old people (assuming that they do not move) maintain their relationship with the church. If people do move, another phenomenon can take place: unconscious annoyance at the "domination" of the church comes to the surface and leads to an alienation from the church. Our Dutch experience also includes the many changes since World War II, which on the one hand are valued as necessary, but are also, on the other hand, cause for reproach by many. Here the Dutch experience is not very different from the American experience. The church is accused of making things either too hard or too easy for people. This development—for younger and older people alike—leads to a greater awakening, but the consequences of that awakening are not always the same for everyone. Especially for pastors there is a real problem at this point.

Relationship to Housing

We have already noticed that the housing problem plays a great part when thinking about providing for old people, especially in times of housing shortage and with the proportion of old people in the general population expanding. The building of large homes for the elderly seemed the best solution in many cases. People have changed their minds about that rather quickly.

The general conviction now is that for the sake of their health, and, more generally, their vitality, it is better if older people are exposed, as much as possible, to the stimulus of a bit of daily work. To a great extent living in a separate house provides this.

Something must be added here. We are going to have to be careful to put these houses in peaceful neighborhoods when possible. Modern traffic is an increasing burden for the aging person. And yet they must be able to reach the homes of children and friends easily: research indicates more and more clearly how important social contacts are for old people.

I also point out that having a place of one's own is especially important in connection with the older person's fundamental need for autonomy. Anyone who lends an ear to the concerns of older people in connection with housing will notice that almost invariably they have a great anxiety about losing their freedom and becoming dependent. Here again I see an important parallel to development in the early years. Erikson indicates the need, in the second phase of human development, for autonomy; it is central to this phase of development. The awareness of being able to take care of oneself and of not being dependent is thus a deeply engraved element in human existence. The aging person moves through a major, painful process of giving up cherished objects and physical abilities. Near the end of this process, giving up autonomy may now come to the surface, as if in a reversal of the beginning of life, but the necessity for autonomy is one of the last and deepest needs. We must allow this independence as long as possible. A home of one's own is a symbol for older people; more than that, a proof that they are not yet dependent.

Relationship to the Family

One often has the impression that in a modern industrial society families live in isolation. Families are like little islands surrounded by the sea of modern life. Older people must therefore live in such isolation.

This picture is inaccurate. Research has shown that old people have many contacts with children and other family members. There appears to exist an "extended family network" which sometimes encompasses as many as four generations. This extended family is bound together in all kinds of ways: through financial and other help extended and received, through collective celebrations on birthdays, through regular reunions, and so on. There are old people who are still caring for a ninety-five-year-old father or mother; people in middle age are caring for two sets of grandparents. It is especially the unmarried ones and women in occupations traditionally thought of as having many unmarried women in them, such as nursing and teaching, who are threatened with isolation.

It is certainly clear that for the aging person the family members have a lot to say. One seeks a kind of safety, security. Even in the earliest days of childhood—another parallel with early development—security offers opportunity for the development of basic trust. In security the child develops ego strength. In later years we can also see how grandparents possess a clear concept of identity and self-worth through their contacts with other family members.

It is striking but understandable that families come together at the death and burial of old people. It is as if their departure is experienced as a turning back to the family "womb." Human beings in death turn back, as it were, to the place where they began. Death is like a kind of "prize ceremony" in the gradual turning back toward our origins. Stanley Hall, in his book *Senescence: the Last Half of Life*, calls death a return to the womb.

There is, as I see it, still another aspect to the relationship between older people and their families. The British psychiatrist Donald Winnicott has pointed out in a number of important publications how children, at a particular point in their development, find support in "transitional objects." These are objects—dolls, teddy bears, blankets—which they often take to bed in order to sleep better. They are also objects which in some way represent the mother who has gone away when the child lies down to sleep; by means of these objects she leaves behind a bit of warmth and security. We recognize these transitional objects in times of grief, when the umbrella in the hallway or the jacket hanging on the hook still "stands for" the dead person, delaying the process of letting go while at the same time making it possible. Keeping portraits and recalling memories have the same function.

As a reaction to the gradual isolation of old age and to the difficulties in the process of letting go, the contacts with children and grandchildren are a kind of transitional object. They provide a bit of warmth and even security which contacts with neighbors cannot give. They bring to life, as it were, the "bosom of the family." I also wonder whether turning to the past, the willingness to tell how things used to be and sometimes seeking out old places and old acquaintances long absent may not have the same function. One feels oneself at home in the past. If this is the case, then turning toward the past slows down the process of letting go on the one hand (one enjoys what one is experiencing), and on the other hand serves as a support for the process. The jacket hanging on the hook becomes less important in the course of time; thus it has helped complete a developmental process. The same goes for the doll and the teddy bear; the child grows out of them. In the same way the aging person grows toward the end by means of his memories. We turn again to the relationship to the past, and yet we report that in this way the totality of the life cycle is experienced by the aging person. For the achievement of the integrity that Erikson describes, that is important.

An important element in the relationship to the family is the role that the old person can play as grandparent. In the collection already mentioned, *Middle Age and Aging,* Bernice L. Neugarten and Karol K. Weinstein discuss this in an article entitled "The Changing American Grandparent." It is an article worth reading and meaningful for us. They give the results of a research project with seventy pairs of grandparents, in which the subject of interviews was the relationship between grandparent and grandchild.

Some of their more interesting conclusions:

1. In the interviews the degree of comfort in the role was always in the foreground. It seemed that most subjects felt comfortable with it. But about a third had difficulties with the role. As positive aspects of the role, people reported:

a. One stays young, and one sees in the grandchildren the extension of the family

b. To be a grandparent offers emotional fulfillment; one now has time for things one could not do with one's own children, and there is a kind of generativity in that

c. To be a grandparent offers the possibility of being a "teacher" and a "resource person"; one can teach the grandchildren about all kinds of things and can lay aside some money for their future

d. One gets the satisfaction that the grandchildren achieve, and which one did not achieve oneself; there is thus a kind of aggrandizing of the ego.

The one third who did not feel at home in the role of grandparent noted that they did not feel emotionally attached to their grandchildren. They were "too small" or "too busy."

2. The second point brought up in the interviews was the style people used as grandparents. Here, too, there were several possibilities:

a. grandparents who play out their role *formally*, who for example give presents on birthdays, but who do not allow themselves to be drawn into the life and upbringing of the grandchild

b. "fun-seekers" who more than anything else tried to be playmates for their grandchildren

c. a number of grandmothers often functioned as surrogate mothers, especially when the mother worked outside the home

d. grandfather is sometimes the reservoir of the family wisdom

e. grandparents who were genuinely interested in their grandchildren but who, like Santa Claus, were visible only at festival events.

3. The authors of the article conclude by observing that because there are more and more young grandparents (a modern phenomenon) certain roles (such as those mentioned in 2c and 2d) will not be performed, and entering into the grandparent role, the comparatively young people will certainly bring complications with it.

Relationships with One's Own Body

The relationship to the body plays a big role in the experienced world of the aging person. Older people are reminded more than younger people that they not only *are* bodies but that they also *have* bodies. There are two sciences in particular which have to do with the problems that require attention here: medicine and philosophical anthropology. In recent years there has been a great deal of research among physicians into the phenomena associated with the aging process. But for the experienced world of the aging person these have only indirect meaning. Therefore we shall not explore these in any depth. What has more meaning for us is what comes from the side of philosophical anthropology about the body. I think specifically of what Simone de Beauvoir reveals in her book about old age. There are two lines of thought in relation to the body and aging that we can explore with profit.

The first line of thought has to do with the fact that in old age the body *reports,* so to speak. In French existentialism, for example with Sartre, it is a fundamental idea that in ordinary life the body is really not there. That is to say, the body and its activities are so self-evident that we do not notice them; in daily experience the body is *passed over*.

We only become aware of our bodies when they bother us with pain or when they refuse to serve us because something is wrong.

For old people it is common that negative experiences with the body occur. They are thus reminded that they have a body, but not only that; they are made aware by this reminder that the body will fail them within the foreseeable future and that they need to prepare for "taking down their sails" and for a definite end. Rheumatism and hardening of the arteries are ominous words for many people.

The experiences that we aging people have with our bodies, our pains, our frustrations, the boundaries to what we can do, are all reminders that we are on our way to the end. Munnichs sees it as realistic that an elderly person should be confronted with the finitude of his existence. Well, by means of our bodies this confrontation is largely realized. One can even say that one gets used to it.

What we encounter with many old people in relation to the body is an anxiety that because they must "strike their sails" they will lose their *dignity*. Simone de Beauvoir, both in her book about old age and in her beautiful book about the death of her mother, *Une Morte Très Douce*, brings out this anxiety. In fact there are, or were, a number of illnesses that attack our dignity; rheumatism was once the cause of all kinds of bodily deformations. But nowadays medical knowledge can in many cases prevent this. What often frightens many old people in our present time is the possibility of losing their minds; they experience this possibility as a real attack on their dignity. Psychiatrists wonder if people really have to see it this way. Patients themselves have less trouble with this than do those around them. Behind this anxiety I suspect in many people the influence of stoicism in our Western society: the need for keeping to a ("middle") norm or ideal of humanity in everything having to do with the body or the emotions. Often enough that is a good idea and deserves our approval. But it can often also lead to a kind of emotional spasticity and thus carry us toward a certain avoidance of being a body or permitting ourselves to feel pain.

The second line of thought about the relationship to one's body that comes up in connection with aging is whether one is ready to accept the process to which one's body is obviously subject. In other words, whether, having a body, we can come to the point of letting go of it. In relation to the body we can also talk about a grief process. We can understand that not every person can come to this letting go happily. One must finally come to an attitude fed by deeper springs. If this does not happen, one is stuck with rancor or at best with resignation.

What we often notice is that from the body itself a need becomes noticeable, so to speak, which responds to the necessity of letting go. Freud's thought, that there is in nature a primal urge to turn back to the basic situation of rest and death, is, I am convinced, affirmed here. There is in the human psyche a longing for "retirement," to be allowed to rest, to be alone. This is not just true for men; we see in aging women a great need, after a busy life, to be allowed to have a few years of restful existence. This longing for rest is in reality a yielding to a need of the body; right at this point we human beings are a psycho-physical unity. Freud says of this need that he posits not only a "death instinct" but also a love instinct, a life-affirming principle. Well, it is the young years when this "eros" predominantly makes itself felt.

We may say that it belongs to the wisdom of aging to recognize this need for rest deep in oneself and to accept it. This does not need to exclude the idea that we are still acquainted with eros in old age, the need to join in; but this engagement is one which is damped down by the need for rest, and is an engagement at a distance.

Sexuality and Eros in Aging

About this subject there exists in our society a rather stereotyped picture of old people: the aging have no sexual needs or problems. Or perhaps we should say that we don't expect it of them. This is as true for family members of old people as it is for those who have professional dealings with them, such as physicians, social workers, and the administrators of nursing homes. The result is that when we are confronted with the sexuality of old people, we are quickly ready with such labels as "dirty old man." In our image of old people sexuality is not essential; if it appears to be present, it must at least be without passion; it is not necessary. What lies behind this image? Probably a bit of Victorian prudery; for many people sexuality is still "dirty" and physical pleasure suspect, particularly as the years go by. We cannot imagine that old couples would find it pleasant to take a bath together or go to bed together, even though it happens. The root, I think, lies deeper than mere prudery; we cannot escape the oedipal problem in relationships between generations. Aging people should not have any sexuality; they are too old; it is "not right." If one reads Simone de Beauvoir, one can feel how she struggles with just this problem. Against this background it is understandable that not so long ago in homes for the aged married couples were kept apart. But what is the reality? Empirical research tells us that:

a. sexual intercourse continues among the elderly up to old age, even into the eighties. There is a reduction in potency, of the ability to have an erection, but regular intercourse makes continuation possible to an advanced age. Besides ordinary intercourse there is quite often masturbation, particularly among widowers. In addition, many women experience clear sexual urges to an advanced age.

b. sexuality occurs in other than "normal," genital forms, as well. Freud opened our eyes to childish forms of sexuality (which he called perversions). Such forms also occur among the old. They tell off-color jokes, are curious, look at pictures, and may have an inclination toward pedophilia. That is to say, the aging person remains *human*, lives *in* nature, not above it.

A clearly positive attitude toward sexuality is growing in our society; it is reasonable to extend this positive attitude toward sexuality among the elderly.

Alongside this there is another phenomenon which may well be more important than sexuality: friendships between old people of opposite sexes, which have a more or less erotic quality. There are vital old people who go to the theater or to concerts together, and who, even in homes for the aged, do many things together while maintaining their freedom. These friendships mean a great deal to those who participate in them. The eros in them is, I think, more important than any possible sex. When I use the word "eros," I use it in the sense used by Spranger in his *Psychologie des Jugendalters* to talk about adolescents.

He does not exclude sexual components—they play a part in the background and may in fact lead to a certain emotional confusion—but the most important thing in such relationships is the possibility of companionship, of valuing others, of exchanging experiences, with the feeling of being understood and of finding a bit of emotional security. Thinking in terms of Erikson's understanding of development, it can be said that the adolescent undergoes some first tender experiences in intimacy at this point, which will unfold more broadly and deeply later. These friendships among old people might be called a "second bloom" of intimacy. If so, then we would see another parallel to development in earlier years.

Relationship to the Past

In various ways our past plays a role in our lives; two of those are, I think, important for our study.

a. First of all, we have a relationship to the past in the sense that Heidegger discusses in *Being and Time.* He indicates that to be human is to be always "on the way," which means that we come out of a past and direct ourselves toward a future. The past is therefore something that we have behind us, and yet in our consciousness it is still with us and continues with us as we move ahead. Johan Huizinga's formulation that history is the form we use to give an account of our past implies that we are therefore thinking about the future. We give an account of our past with an eye on something, namely the future.

The curious thing about being old is that there is indeed a relationship to the past, but the aging person cannot bring the past into touch with the future. For old people who are confronted with the end of their existence there is no past that can be brought in touch with a future that makes sense, and even less any future connected with the present and a continuation of the past. And yet, as we all know from experience, it is obvious that old people are often busy with their past. They think a great deal about it and gladly talk about it. One may ask what lies behind that. A need to round off one's life? But what does rounding off one's life mean?

b. Simone de Beauvoir points out another way in which the past plays a part in our existence. The past is present in our lives as a number of objective "interests," like a book that we once wrote that now lies before us, a thing we've built and which now must be given the once-over, a plan that we have made which has now taken on its own life. In her book about old age, she writes, "All that I have done my past takes over. It supersedes everything, and takes on a practically inert form. . . . The books I've written have that almost inert quality; they are now my works, they exist apart from me, and identify me as their author. . . . Everyone comes in his work to this kind of objectification in the world and becomes alienated from it." The curious thing is that this inert mass arouses obvious emotions among the aging. A kind of nostalgia comes over them when they are confronted with it. They want to experience it all over again. And they talk about it, as they get older. Especially for early experiences will they sometimes have a sharp memory, which often stands over against difficulty in remembering more recent events. Are some of the nerve pathways not yet worn out?

We get the clearest picture of the meaning of these memories if we see them as a kind of "transitional object," with the purpose of holding on to blurring emotions, and thus of supporting a grief process. Toward the end of the last phase of life we feel a strong need for warmth and security. It gives us a kind of "basic trust" that makes life worth living. Seeking out the important places of one's youth and talking once more with old acquaintances meets this need.

One consequence of this turning back toward the past is a

kind of "coming home" in one's life cycle, as we have already noted. It is a feeling of experiencing life as something complete. One does not live merely within this last phase of life, but within the whole picture. One comes to a reconciliation with one's life cycle and brings the whole picture to life. Making a whole of life, bringing in unconscious processes as well, and being confronted with the fact of an end to the whole thing, helps to let go, helps to make the grief process complete. There comes a feeling of closing things out, rounding things off.

More or less connected with this is a need to "evaluate," to give an account of the worthwhileness of it all. It is not just the question, What have we accomplished? that is important, but also such questions as: Do we feel attached to it in a positive way? Was it good? Are we grateful for it? Life becomes, when we look back on it as older people, not just a stream of more or less accidental incidents, but a unified whole to which we have been attached, which happened to us, about which we had expectations and for which we made plans. In the long run, it was something nhat we in part created. We made choices, we had a certain attitude, it was the result of a project on our part. To live is to have experienced much and to have done much. And now, looking back on it and calling up our memories of it once again, it becomes *our* painting, *our* life.

Two questions come to the fore: Was it good, were we happy? and Was it a success? Can we be satisfied? It is the answer to these two questions which in the polarity integrity *vs.* disgust/despair decides the issue in this last phase of life. It is as though there is present in the background the concept that life is something once put into our hands but which we now must give back. And that sets us thinking about how it was and with what feelings we are giving it back. In succeeding chapters we shall see this aspect of the aging person's relationship with the past more closely.

One last comment. In all kinds of books about aging emphasis is put on the idea that one of the central aspects of aging is finding a relationship with one's past. Yet a deeper insight into what older people seek and experience in that relationship is missing in many views of old age. We can also see this preoccupation with what lies behind us as a part of a grief process in which they are involved. Is it not also an attempt to integrate into our lives in a new way the worthwhile things that are now past and that we must now let go? The study of grief makes it clear that "letting go" is something that must happen in order for new attachments to take place. But just as important—or more important—in any grief process is that we learn to be attached, in a new, free, and grateful way, to what we have lost. We have paid too little attention to this aspect up to now, but this is what aging people are doing when they are so busy with all their memories.

Relationship to Death

Death poses difficult problems for people in any society. It awakens deep emotions with which people do not know how to cope. Our present society is marked by the fact that after an earlier taboo against talking about death and dying there is now serious talking and thinking about these themes. In therapeutic and pastoral circles there is much discussion about working with terminal patients. People try to get a psychological "handle" on the experience of death and, from a philosophical perspective, to break through the mysteries of life and death.

In 1970, in response to an invitation from the editors of the Dutch journal *Tijdschrift voor Theologie* to contribute to an issue on the theme "Living in Spite of Death," I wrote an article on "Death in Human Experience." I should like to set out some of the thoughts I found most important in that article. Death, I said then, is a mystery that has two aspects: the same two aspects mentioned by Rudolf Otto many years ago in his book, *The Idea of the Holy*. The first is the *mysterium tremendum* (the terrifying); the second is the *mysterium fascinosum* (the attractive, the fascinating). Human beings "meet" death in two ways in their lives. First of all, in an "acute" form, as something that comes upon us like a reality very nearby. Then one has to deal with the situation described by Kübler-Ross, who describes how people are caught up in a very involved process in which they go through a variety of stages, coming finally to acceptance. The second is that people are aware, more or less clearly, of their mortality. We therefore experience our lives as a "being unto death," and either avoid this or accept it. Martin Heidegger analyzed this basic fact of human existence in his *Being and Time*, and Ernest Becker, in a study entitled *The Denial of Death*, undertook a close analysis of this problem from a more psychological perspective. (He expounded the idea of the human fear of death as the driving force in human affairs.)

This experience of mortality shows that death approaches us in two ways. These are connected to the experience of the *mysterium tremendum et fascinosum* we have just mentioned. We speak on the one hand of the horror of death and of the grave, which means that we experience death as the devourer, the destroyer. It is in this connection that Freud saw a link between anxiety about death and castration anxiety. But on the other hand we speak of the rest that death brings; we speak of the "bosom of the earth" to which we entrust the dead person. As we noted above, Stanley Hall connected the death experience with a return to mother's womb. Many poets have written about death in a similar vein.

We have the clear impression that as an aging person reaches about sixty-five there is a peaking of anxiety about death; it preoccupies the thoughts. In the subsequent years this anxiety drops away gradually, sometimes reaching the point of a longing for the end. It is, I think, this phase of life Hall is describing when he talks about death as a return to the womb. It is a process stretching out over many years and is marked by all kinds of "ups and downs." In old age we also see slowly disappearing the feeling that death is mysterious; people talk quite realistically about their departure and give specific instructions about their burial or their cremation.

Here I think we must ask whether this development may not also have a biological background. If the species is to survive, then individuals have to avoid this idea by means of their anxiety about death. Such a necessity disappears when individuals have completed their task and their end comes into view. We also see animals, when they sense that their end is upon them, seeking a quiet place in which to die. Anxiety about death can, from a biological perspective, disappear as people grow older. In the same way sexuality can eventually disappear when it is no longer necessary. Earlier we saw that sexuality does not fall away completely. What does happen is that the frequency of sexual urges and sexual potency slowly decreases.

It is, then, a normal part of aging that one gradually comes to think less about death, and specifically that the anxiety about it decreases. There exists a growing readiness to give oneself over to death, and in advanced old age this becomes in many cases a positive expectation. (Here I must remind the reader that this is not some kind of law of nature; there are instances where people feel quite differently.) What is striking is that people in general do little concrete thinking about the hereafter. People do fantasize about it, but these fantasies are more projections of certain longings or anxieties than conscious attempts to erect particular theories about life after death.

Finally, I note that when death appears as an immediate possibility on the horizon, it can still bring into play the process that Kübler-Ross describes, with its phases of rebellion and bargaining. But we also know of many cases in which the phase of acceptance is reached quite quickly.

The Experience of Finitude

We have seen that the experience of finitude is one of the most important aspects of aging. The way in which an old person works through the problem of finitude is the key to understanding human beings in this phase of life. We must at this point be clear in our thinking: finitude is not the same as death. The experience of the finitude of existence begins quite early for many people; Rümke has already indicated that the loss of teeth can be experienced by a person in his forties as a sign of the approaching end. For some people it can happen even earlier than that.

Munnichs begins with the position that the experience of finitude leads toward a kind of disengagement and, by means of that, to a renewed engagement but now at a distance. This process is surely present but it is a part of a larger process, that of aging, which we can characterize as a grief process. Now let us look more closely at the work of Munnichs.

His research originally appeared under the title, *Ouderdom en Eindigheid* (*Old Age and Finitude.* Central portions of it were republished as part of a collection of essays on social gerontology. My citations are from that collection.) After reminding the reader that there remains in our culture a taboo on talking about death and dying, he writes: "While the general conception is one of denial and repression, several studies indicate that among old people we will encounter a positive attitude toward the end of life. It is precisely this contrast that raises the question whether there may not be a specific connection between one's age and one's attitude toward death, or the end of existence."

The following questions are central:

—Is the experience of finitude more strongly in the foreground for older people than for younger ones?

—What is the relationship between old age and finitude? Do old people dread finitude or are they familiar with it?

—Can the attitude toward finitude be seen as a point of crystallization in old age, i.e. be taken as a realistic sign of old age?

These three questions are about three different themes: (a) about being busy with the question of finitude, the question of occupation; (b) about the degree of familiarity with finitude; and (c) about the attitude toward finitude. Munnichs directs his inquiry toward these three things and comes up with important conclusions, which I shall recount in his own words. It is admittedly an extended citation, but his writing is too important to be abridged. We shall take them in the reverse order.

With reference to his research on the attitude toward finitude, he says:

1. With the advancing years old people are more often accepting and at peace; to the extent that they are young, they tend more to deny, avoid, and flee.

2. Old people who have had a lot of experience with death are more accepting and at peace.

3. Old people with a positive attitude toward preparations for death are often more accepting and at peace.

4. If one's occupations and needs are fewer in number, one is often more accepting and at rest.

5. Men are accepting and resigned more than women.

6. Widowers are often accepting; elderly married women often use denial and avoidance; widows seldom do.

7. If their children live elsewhere, then old people are seldom accepting and often evasive.

8. If the old person remains in a familiar social milieu, then he/she seldom flees or denies. But if he/she lives alone with a spouse, flight and denial are common.

9. Old people without a sense of having fulfilled a life purpose often use flight and denial.

10. Old people who can be characterized as having one or more crises use denial and flight often.

11. Old people who have two or more "socialization problems" use more flight and denial.

With regard to "familiarity with finitude," here is what Munnichs found:

1. The older people are, the more familiar they are with finitude; the younger, the more it is alien to them.

2. Old people with a positive attitude toward preparations for death are often familiar with finitude. If their opinion is negative, they are seldom familiar with finitude.

3. Widowers are more aware of finitude than married men. The same holds true for widows in comparison with married women. These last are seldom aware of finitude.

4. Old people with more experience of death are familiar with finitude. Old people with limited experience with death ignore finitude more.

5. Old people who live alone ignore finitude often. The same is true if they live alone with a spouse.

6. Old women use avoidance more than old men; for them the idea of finitude is often alien.

7. Old people who have a medium or small amount of contact with their children often use avoidance.

8. When their children live "elsewhere," then old people avoid the idea of finitude.

9. If one's hobbies decrease, finitude becomes strange; if they increase, one tends to use avoidance more frequently.

10. If an old person's social contacts increase, then the person tends to use avoidance; if they decrease, then the old person uses less avoidance.

11. If social needs and problems increase, then the familiarity with finitude decreases and avoidance increases.

12. Old people with a large number of the marks of old age are seldom familiar with finitude.

13. Old people without a sense of fulfillment are seldom familiar with finitude.

In the area of attitude toward and preoccupation with finitude, Munnichs found the following:

1. With advancing years the old person confronts finitude; the younger he is, the less he confronts it.

2. Old people with a lot of experience with death confront (or have confronted) finitude often.

3. If social contacts are increasing, then there is more frequent confrontation with finitude. To the extent that these contacts are less, there is less confrontation.

4. Among widows and widowers whose spouses died five to ten years previously there appears little confrontation with finitude.

5. Persons in distress allow themselves little confrontation with finitude.

6. People without grandchildren confront finitude relatively seldom.

Several things are striking about these three lists. In the first place, there is always a note of *process* during aging. This is quite clear in his writing about the attitude toward finitude where he says "with advancing years . . ." Elsewhere one reads "the older . . ."

The second striking thing is that there are obviously inner and outer factors which influence this process. Munnichs says about this: "Crucial for acceptance and resignation are *the personal view of the old person about death, the circumstances of being old, and the opportunity to work these through (i.e. not to be busy with other things), little need to worry about daily existence, and a pleasant social surrounding.*"

In the process of aging there are thus three factors that have positive meaning:

1. The existence of social contacts, especially with children. We may say, in line with the thinking of Terruwe, that old people receive a kind of security from these contacts, a strengthening of what Erikson calls basic trust. It is also Erikson who brought to light the importance of the surrounding community for the development of the identity concept. Persons know who they are and what they are worth in part from their contacts with the society around them.

2. The possession of a particular viewpoint, an inner attitude. Munnichs, in another place, uses the following words to describe this: sense of reality, courage, maturity, and adulthood.

3. Having no cares, or few of them. Munnichs talks of not having to busy oneself with the "needs of existence." Next to this in meaning is having some experience with death, for example, that of close relatives.

These three factors influence one another and work together to help the old person be able to accept the limitations of his existence; for us the second factor is of particular importance. Munnichs: "By way of conclusion with regard to the old person for whom finitude remains alien, we have already indicated the possible relatedness of limited or scanty engagement, fear, and holding back, which hinder an open dialogue with one's surroundings and one's own experience of life." A number of variations are conceivable here, determined by circumstances. The reverse is true for old people with courage about life. Engagement has been in the foreground for them, and so timely confrontation with finitude has already taken place. The attitude that makes this possible also brings a new dimension to engagement; it now becomes engagement at a distance, which in turn makes possible a new meaning of existence. The courage to live can thus be conceived of as a tendency toward engagement, and as a condition for giving meaning to existence. Anxiety about life is then a tendency toward uncertainty and holding back, which narrow engagement and thereby limit the possibility of a confrontation with finitude. The need for meaning does not even arise in this situation, but there does exist a feeling of unfulfillment.

"By taking another look at the connections [Munnichs writes], it is also possible to deal with the categories of spiritual health and unhealth. Spiritually healthy old people would come to acceptance; spiritually unhealthy people would not know a way to deal with finitude and would rather flee. We should make an observation in connection with these categories which in our view is an unavoidable requirement for reaching a fundamental acceptance, namely, that old people, at least temporarily, waver and stall before the problem of finitude."

Two brief remarks about this: it is important that Munnichs writes in his last sentence that in the process of aging acceptance is linked with ups and downs. Several times now, we have called this a grief process. And of course in a grief process we also recognize the different phases through which a person must go. We also recognize that the basic terms that Munnichs uses here, such as engagement, courage of life, and the giving of meaning, are all rather vague. It is difficult to fill them with clear content. Yet it is clear that he is referring to something real with these words.

What Munnichs further writes is also important: "It is clearly possible to read from the figures that, of those who flee from and are not familiar with finitude, nor think much about it, the largest number are in the age group 70-74. Denial exhibits in the figures . . . a constant decline and has even disappeared in the oldest group in the study, as have flight, unfamiliarity, and refusal to think about finitude.

For the moment, Munnichs wants to keep as only a hypothesis what his research shows: that there is a manifest increase (over time) of acceptance and familiarity and willingness to deal with finitude. He prefers to think of it as a proposition to be tested by further research. We notice that between seventy and seventy-four there seems to be a critical phase through which aging people must go. We do need to understand that Munnichs' research did not concern itself with people under seventy.

In all of this one important question is the extent to which religion exercises an influence on the inner attitudes of aging people in the process they are going through. It seems that in order to answer this question we shall have to know what sort of religion is meant. Munnichs often sees a *formal* religion which does not lead to any acceptance. He cites the example of Mrs. L: "With Mrs. L we are talking about a readiness to flee. She is afraid; it is an anxiety that she wants to stave off and destroy by religious means."

Munnichs apparently assumes that something other than this formal religiosity leads to a better inner attitude. He names a number of conditions that must be fulfilled if one wants to come to an acceptance of finitude. Thus one must have confronted oneself and have learned to accept one's own limitations. He names as a third condition (and a very important one for us) that one must have given some sort of meaning to finitude. He suggests that there is a connection between developing a meaning and looking over one's life. One must have a view of the life through which one has lived. He speaks in this connection of a call from the far side of death, something outside of the grasp of empirical knowledge, which nonetheless leaves no doubt about its effect.

I want to dwell on this point somewhat more. Several questions suggest themselves. It seems as though Munnichs identifies religion with a belief in immortality, or sees it as inseparably tied to it. Is this the case? And does religion have an influence on the acceptance and working through of the concept of finitude by means of factors other than hope and expectation? Munnichs writes that old people often make a connection between their view of life and their attitude toward finitude. This view of life can be religious, generally humanist, or vaguely philosophical, a sort of general "looking at life." This philosophy often consists of several stereotypical and impersonal remarks which represent a sort of "life balance."

An analysis of his material teaches Munnichs that one can subdivide these attributions of meaning reported by old people into seven categories:

1. An explicitly religious attribution of meaning, personally experienced
2. An explicitly humanistic attribution of meaning, personally experienced
3. An implicit attribution of meaning, personally experienced, whether religious or humanistic
4. An ambivalent attitude with regard to religion, thus an attitude of belief and unbelief together
5. A formally religious attribution
6. Stereotypical remarks
7. No meaning given at all.

Munnichs gives examples of each category from his material. Then he researches what the connection is between these categories and the attitude toward the end of one's existence. He finds a large group which gives an explicitly religious meaning to things, and which accepts finitude. Second, there is a large group which gives an implicitly religious or humanistic meaning, and which accepts finitude. After that there are three smaller groups: (a) those who accept finitude and give it a humanistic meaning, (b) those who are resigned and who give to finitude an implicitly religious or humanistic meaning, and (c) those who evade finitude and give evidence of a formally religious understanding. Two things are striking in this analysis. First, one can come to acceptance through a generally humanistic understanding; a religious understanding is not decisively necessary. Second, a formally religious understanding can lead toward an avoidance of coming to grips with finitude. That is an important statement for us.

At the end of his essay Munnichs briefly discusses the question, Which is primary, one's attitude toward finitude or the meaning one gives to it? From his data it appears that in by far the most instances the meaning one gives to finitude is of profound influence on the attitude one takes toward it; the meaning conditions the attitude, and not the other way around. Only in a few special cases is the attitude primary and the meaning secondary. This is also an important piece of data for us.

To close this review of Munnichs' essay, this note. When I make the connection between religion and his use of meaning, the word "meaning" strikes me as inadequate to describe what really must be observed in the life and behavior of religious people. The word "meaning" suggests a process of a primarily intellectual and verbal character, but in the quotations that Munnichs uses the emphasis is primarily laid upon feelings. For the religious person a deep trusting, of the kind that Erikson calls "basic trust," is the primary thing. We need a more psychodynamically oriented "X-ray" to get a good picture of what is at stake for older people.

Here I think we run up against an important problem in the otherwise valuable work of Munnichs. It seems that he has no clear and satisfying theory to get at the underlying questions which his research raises. He speaks about an experience of finitude which leads to an acceptance of it. But by what process within the personality the aging person can come to such an acceptance is a question that remains dim. He indicates that having social contacts, possessing a particular point of view, an inner attitude, and not being burdened with cares all play a part, but we get no insight into the psychological dynamics of this process.

Acceptance of finitude also leads, as he sees it, to a "disengagement," but here again it is not clear by what process this takes place within the ego. The same holds true of the shift from this disengagement to a renewed engagement at a distance. We must therefore ask if these shifts indicated by Munnichs can be made any clearer.

My own thoughts tend in the direction of a view of aging as an "unfastening process," which means a certain kind of grief process. Munnichs does speak of an anticipated separation. I will come back to this in chapter 8. Here I want to say, however, that Munnichs has indicated key problems, but that we need other theories and conceptions to get at a deeper understanding of these problems. There are, moreover, still other phenomena among the aged which he has not dealt with adequately, such as their preoccupation with the past, their need for an evaluation of their life cycle, and what Erikson includes in the concept of Integrity. These questions, too, need clarification and a more inclusive theory.

Finally, we note that Munnichs writes that many old people, according to his research, stay stuck with problems about finitude. He writes: "We must therefore conclude that a relatively large number of old people do not approach a meaning or opinion about finitude, in other words that they do not experience an old age worthy of a human being. Consequently there is, humanly speaking, a much greater tragedy than is commonly presumed. On the basis of what we have said, we do not doubt that this tragedy is not sufficiently connected with the attitude toward human finitude that we can see as a touchstone for a fully achieved maturity."

For those who deal with old people and bear a definite responsibility toward them this is an important conclusion.

7

The World as the Aging Person Experiences It (Continued)

This chapter is a continuation of the description of the experienced world of the aging person begun in the previous chapter. We concerned ourselves in the last chapter with their relationships to the world around them and to certain aspects of life such as their relationships with the past, with death, and with finitude; now we want to concentrate on aging as a process personally lived through. We begin with their relationship with religion.

The Relationship with Religion

In the area of the religious life of older people images once again play a role. In one of my congregations an aging man, whose aged father had died, once said to me, "When you age you ought to come home to the church." We all know from the press about non-religious public and political figures who, as the years advance, know how to find their way back to the church and the sacraments. Again and again we come up against communist or fascist dictators who try to come to some kind of cooperation with the church, who want to reserve to themselves the "ownership" of people during their lifetimes and then to hand them over to the church as the end of life approaches. Many see the task of the church as standing by people in their struggles with the problems of mortality, and preparing them for the hereafter. Religion is thus a knowledge of mortality and a preparation for dying; it is thus primarily something for older people.

This image is not supported by the facts. It is most of all in early adolescence that we can find a heightened religious interest; that is also the period in which the greatest number of conversions takes place. Moreover, according to research, relatively little thought is given by old people to a life after death; the preoccupation with finitude does not always lead to thinking about the hereafter. There is to be sure an interest in what will possibly happen to people after death, but, seen more closely, this appears to be an expression of understandable human curiosity, not tied to a person's age or a particular hallmark of specific religious groups; a person's age seems to be an incidental factor.

Munnichs pays some attention to the question of the extent to which older people are concerned with the hereafter. He thinks that "in the phase of aging and old age human beings face the necessity of accepting not only the limits posed by finitude, but also what comes after that, which remains in fact invisible and unknown." He says that people come to this acceptance in the same way they come to accept finitude, namely, through a certain maturity. According to him, the attribution of meaning, whether of a religious or a humanistic sort, plays a large part. As I have said, I do not know whether this word "meaning" is the happiest choice, but Munnichs is certainly pointing in a good direction. One might perhaps better speak of ego strength or of basic trust. Maturity creates, as Munnichs puts it, "a security which is a defense against the uncertainty of what can or must come after the end." In other words, the trust that a person possesses in this life will also be valid for what comes later. I recognize that trust in the words of Han Fortmann on his deathbed: "Whoever has once met God finds the question of the hereafter no longer interesting. He who has learned to live in the High Light is not troubled by the question whether the Light will still be there in the morning. It never occurs to the child that lives under the tender care of its mother to ask whether mother will be there tomorrow."[1] I have often encountered this maturity or basic trust in my pastoral practice. "Maturity" thus means that on the basis of one's belief one also accepts the insecurity of the hereafter; one lets the question alone. One can describe this "belief" as an attitude toward life based on either religious or humanistic considerations; in the last analysis one can in certain situations even speak of hope.

But what we must not forget is that here the kind of belief is of primary significance. Not all belief, not even that of old people, can be judged positively. Adorno and his colleagues have distinguished two kinds of belief in their book, *The Authoritarian Personality*,[2] and Allport has made the same distinction in his book, *The Nature of Prejudice*.[3] We need to talk about mature and immature belief. Immature belief has a defensive function for human beings; people who are too anxious to allow themselves to grow cling to it. The content of this belief is conventional in nature; it is conformist in character and has an institutional flavor to it. Over against that stands what may be called mature belief, which does not close itself off from new possibilities and new meanings. It exercises a wholly different function in human life: the energizing of the personality. The content of this belief rests on one's own value judgments. It is not conformist but instead it is independent and gives evidence of a personally acquired and lived piety.

We can distinguish these two sorts of belief among older people. There are old people who, in their beliefs as in everything else, are defensive, who try to use their belief to protect themselves against insecurity and anxiety, as well as from that which from the outside makes them insecure and anxious. Over against them stand old people who keep on growing, who accept new possibilities and the uncertainties that go with them, indeed welcome them: people who remain open and do not feel threatened. Adorno suggests that experiences in early youth are of great influence in the formation of these two attitudes.

In an article entitled "Religiosity in Old Age" appearing in the collection already named, *Middle Age and Aging*, David O. Moberg gives a good overview of the current status of research on this subject.[4] He distinguishes five different dimensions: the experiential, the ideological, the ritualistic, the intellectual, and the consequential. Under these headings he discusses what happens to old people. With regard to religious feelings the results of research are unclear. There are researchers who find no evidence for the proposition that people become more religious as they age, while others come to the opposite conclusion. As far as religious convictions are concerned, research indicates that older people are more conservative than younger ones. In the area of religious practices—going to church and other aspects of the ritual dimension—findings are not consistent. Church attendance remains rather constant except for the very old who often have physical difficulties, but it is doubtful that we can connect church attendance and personal piety. What *is* striking, however, is that participation in other social organizations diminishes more rapidly than participation in church life. In the intellectual area there exists no research, although as far as the effects of religious life are concerned, it is clear that older people who remain active in church life are in general better adapted than others; but here more research is necessary. Moberg sums up with several global conclusions. The first is that there is something like disengagement in aging people on the one hand, specifically in the area of church participation, but at the same time we see a reengagement, in the sense that there is a sort of intensification in feelings and convictions; older people tend to experience their faith more personally.

A few remarks about this. If it is true that aging is a grief process, aging can lead aging people to seek a "handhold" in a conventional, fundamentalistically colored religion; but through confrontation with essential life questions it can also lead to a process of inner change and in fact to growth; this results in a call to a capacity for hope and love by which people can come to a deep acceptance and a faithful belief. People then seem in a position to let go of all kinds of side issues, possibly many conceptions and propositions, and to concentrate on the elements which have their roots in basic trust. In that way they also find, as it were, their identity as old people. We all know the type of old person who lives in this way. Such a person represents an ideal for us: the person who knows the relative values of things and who gives evidence of a certain deeply founded wisdom born out of a commitment to the tasks which this phase of life sets for us.

One more remark: I have encountered in the literature no description of the old person whom I have met several times in my pastoral work: the person who tries to work everything out through a process of rational search. This person reads a great deal, is a regular attender of all kinds of lectures and conferences, and is looking, so to speak, for a light on the background questions of human existence, and sometimes in esoteric or occult circles. My impression is that we find such people among former dogmatic believers.

Relationships with Ourselves

The concept of self is one of the difficult concepts in psychology. It is not possible to give a good definition of it or to develop a satisfactory theory of it. We may say that ideas about self move in two directions.

The first direction is that of anthropological theory. The self is for the anthropologist an aspect of a fixed structure and stands as such in opposition to the ego. Professor L. van der Horst writes, for example: "In the human being we always come into contact with two sets of ideas . . . . next to my "ego" as a free, creative power is all of that which can be an object for my consciousness, everything that the human person *has* and which belongs to him: the body, the life story, the historical totality. My life story in this sense is *my* creation."

Then there is the direction in which the self is an aspect of a movement in the ego; the ego is seen here as being on the road toward being more and deeper, and the self is in that connection the ideal, the end point of that movement. The ego wants to become, must become, a self.

This second direction is the most important for our study. Let me then approach the question of the relation of the ego and the self more closely and then move to the situation created by psychoanalysis in this area.

Freud's great discovery was the concept of an unconscious, determined part of life alongside conscious life. Parallel to this distinction is the one between an infantile ego and a mature ego which is in a better condition to accept reality than the infantile ego. But he did not work out the problem of the relationship between the ego and the self, he brought it to light. He places an accent on the fact that the ego must grow through the solution of problems which it has brought with it as unfinished business from childhood. The ego must become adult, i.e. it must grow toward more freedom and independence, and especially must learn to accept reality. Then the ego becomes more itself.

With his non-directive method of psychotherapy Rogers takes Freud's line of thought farther; with him, too, the emphasis is on the need (really more: on the longing) of the ego to grow, and, as with Freud, through the solution of "unfinished business." More with Rogers than with Freud is there emphasis on the appeal made in the therapeutic relationship to become independent. The ego really becomes itself when it comes to decisions for which it wants to be responsible itself. It is as if for Rogers the self slumbers in the depths of human existence and comes awake in the warmth and space of the therapeutic relationship. Jung must also be seen as an inheritor of Freud. For him the personal unconscious is embedded in the collective unconscious, but just as with Freud the ego becomes more itself through the development of consciousness, through the solution of unfinished business. This solution is at the same time an integration, no longer a repression, but an admitting and a learning to live with it. In images, Jung says it this way: that human beings are accompanied by a shadow that they do not at first want to see, but which they must integrate into themselves if they are to become themselves. The ego grows, it goes through—to use Jung's words—an individuation process, but in this process it becomes richer and deeper. In the person who has become himself or herself, the animus and anima (male and female principles respectively) no longer stand over against each other but form a polarized unity.

So-called humanistic psychology, such as that of Maslow or the Gestalt psychologists, stands in the same line in its own way. The ego becomes more itself through realizing its hidden possibilities. It is led to this through a set of hierarchical needs. By becoming itself in this way, the ego receives a certain breadth and depth. This growth also involves a liberation from having to take on a certain masculine or feminine role or from being bound to certain attitudes, e.g. of the body, which do not suit the ego. So here, too, the relationship between the ego and self is marked by a certain growth toward more inner freedom, toward independence, and toward greater depth.

When we talk thus about the relation to the self we move toward a rather clearly fenced off area in which the differing directions in psychology accentuate particular aspects.

Now, what has this to do with old people? What can we say about their relationships to themselves? That this is a useful question is evidenced by the fact that Munnichs says at several critical points that if we wish to be old in the right way we have to possess a certain ripeness or maturity and that Erikson indicates that it is the task of people in this life phase to come to a certain integrity. Older people, then, too, can be themselves to a greater or lesser degree.

Our beginning point is that the same problems and structures pertain to old people as to others. With them, as with others, we can be up against the opposites of conscious and unconscious, relieved and repressed, infantile and adult, mature and immature. Modern psychology has opened our eyes to the fact that we live in a swinging balance between two behavior patterns, a balance concerned in its depths with the will toward maturing and self-actualization. How that balance looks is connected with the character or personality formed during the course of our lives, and especially in our formative years. We all recognize the trail of unfinished business. This goes for old people, too. They too have unfinished business. They can be dependent and anxious, aggressive, and struggling with feelings of loneliness and shortcomings; in brief, they are not always, in the deepest sense of the word, inwardly free. What we must never forget is that old people have a life behind them and that this life has left its traces upon them.

What is important is that we recognize, from developmental psychology, that these two patterns become visible in each developmental phase in the confrontation with the particular task that the phase carries with it. Erikson is the primary person who has opened our eyes to the different tasks in each developmental phase.

The question is, With what task are old people in this phase of their lives confronted? As we have seen, Munnichs puts it that the old person is confronted with the end of his existence and thus comes to a disengagement. His task, we may say, is to let go, to come to some removal of the stitches; he must, to use Freud's phraseology, take his libido back. One can also say that his task is to acknowledge his finitude, to accept the fact that he is on his way to the end, to death. In an interview in the church journal *Hervormd Nederland,* the psychotherapist Dr. H. R. Wijngaarden was asked about his experiences of aging. What is striking about his response is the words he used with some detachment: worked up, difficult, make sad, embarrass, compensate, anxious dashing about, rebelling; all of them point to the inner difficulties which can be associated with aging. Munnichs talks about an anticipated separation. Psychologists speak of anticipatory grief, thus indicating a grief for which one is preparing oneself, a loss that one is not yet undergoing, but which one knows is approaching. This process of anticipatory or preparatory grief is certainly applicable to aging people. The basic problem before which such people stand is whether they are ready for such a grief process. This is really the subject at which Munnichs' research is aimed. We know from psychology that such a grief process is one of the most fundamental emotional processes through which human beings go. Are we ready to rip out the seams, remove the stitches? We know, from studies of the mother-child relationship, how difficult this undoing can be and the problems it can raise for both mother and child. Harlow made the same discovery in his research with monkeys. Reality requires of the growing person that he learn to live in an ever more real way, i.e. without fleeing to mother's bosom, and on the foundation of a basic trust woven out of the contact with the mother. But that almost never happens without tension. In later grief processes we see how denial, anger, despair, and depression are often the phases through which one must struggle, if one wants to push through to that basic trust and get in touch with the kernel of reality, so as to freely recognize that life is good.

So we can formulate it this way: the task before which human beings come to stand in this period of life is to come, by means of a process which is really a grief process, to a basic trust, thus to belief, acceptance, and hope. And the problem is whether we are ready to do that.

Against the background of this question we begin to realize what Munnichs means by adulthood and maturity, and what Erikson means by *integrity*. We remember that the development of integrity is what Erikson posits as the developmental task for human beings in the last phase of life. Let us stop for a moment at this concept, and let me quote Erikson. Integrity, he says, is "the acceptance of one's one and only unique life cycle as something that had to be and which could not be otherwise. It therefore means a new and different love for one's parents, free of the wish that they might have been different, and an acceptance of the fact that one's life is one's own responsibility . . . the person who has integrity is ready to defend the worth of his own life style against all physical and economic threats. . . . But the end of the life cycle brings to life 'final questions' in relation to the problem of what chance a person can have to overcome the limitations of his identity and his often tragic or bitterly tragicomic setting in his one and only life. . . . Great philosophical and religious systems . . . seek this victory through letting go but are at the same time ethically concerned for the salvation of the world. . . . Psychological strength, we conclude, rests on an all-inclusive process that orders individual life cycles, the succession of generations, and the structure of society all at the same time."[5]

In these quotations, Erikson lays clear emphasis on the acceptance of one's parents and of oneself, and thus of several fundamental factors connected with basic trust. But if one listens carefully to what he says one hears in his words the necessity for the older person to be reconciled to his own life and life cycle. He writes that at the end of one's life one is confronted with a new identity crisis which can be formulated with the words, "I am that which survives me."[6] These words stand against the background of his observations about the fundamental meaning of society and the succession of generations. In the depth of our being we know that self-acceptance is only possible on the basis of knowing oneself to be accepted. This is what the great religions have expressed in their belief in a hereafter; it has less to do, I think, with a need to keep on living or to be immortal (even though that may not be separable from it) as with the deep need, at the end of life, to be acceptable and accepted.

What comes through here is a general human need that every child knows in relation to its parents, that is carried through into adult life in society, and that at the end of life we look for from our ancestors and our descendants. In the evaluation of the life cycle through which every aging person goes at least unconsciously, the question, Am I in this life cycle acceptable? plays a hidden but traceable role. It is therefore quite understandable that in the religious sphere one thinks about God and that in so doing in connection with the end of the life cycle and specifically with death there are many texts and rituals such as last confessions and the righting of wrongs, all of which point to the problem of acceptability. One can even say that the gospel can come to mind with its promise that one is acceptable not on the basis of having earned it but on the basis of God's forgiving love.

So we conclude that in Erikson's integrity concept the idea is present that one finds one's life cycle acceptable.

Behind this are other meanings. If one wishes to be responsible for the purpose of one's life then one must on the one hand be ready to enter into human life, but on the other hand be ready at the end of life to step out again. I recognize that these words sound somewhat "pretty" and therefore do not always correspond to our feelings in relation to our own existence, but I also believe that we are in touch here with the deepest motives that are decisive for the happy rounding off of a human life. It is a part of the success of a life that one sees oneself as one who has a part in the parade of generations; life is something which does not stop with us but which must be continued and which has a future after our own end.

If we look at the aging process from the viewpoint of libido theory we can see another important factor. One can illuminate the grief process by saying that libido is withdrawn from the lost object with the aim of (after a time) being free for investment in a new object. After a death one cannot immediately invest love in another person; it requires time. If being old involves, as we have seen that it does, a grief process, in which one lets go, comes to a disengagement, then one can ask where the freed libido goes. There are no new objects toward which it can direct itself. The only object remaining is the person herself. A small warning is appropriate here; the disengagement is of course not total. It directs itself toward work, performance. Releasing oneself from human relationships comes only much later and has a different character. So we must say that the new love object is the person himself in the surroundings of family and friends to which he is connected. The picture that we get from Munnichs of the aging person is that such a person is indeed concerned with himself and the people he loves. To use psychoanalytic language, there is a certain narcissism. I note here that this concept has partially lost its negative meaning; one speaks nowadays of healthy narcissism. We may posit a healthy narcissism among many old people.

One particular aspect of this is that they are in a position to "enjoy," which means that they are in a position to satisfy a number of primary longings. They are very much involved with themselves in a positive way. We must also note, however, that being occupied with oneself can also take place in a negative way, which can lead to grumbling and to self-pity. But the renewed engagement of which Munnichs speaks clearly has the flavor of positive narcissism. It involves being busy with a number of things that now without the demands of one's job people find pleasant: hobbies, nature, art (particularly being creative oneself), and grandchildren.

In the grief process of aging, good communication is of great importance. We have already indicated several times the danger of isolation among old people. From everything we know it seems that having good and regular social contacts is of great importance for them—thus it is important that children live not too far away, so that regular contact with them is possible.

Having such contacts gives aging people an identity; they have their own place in a larger whole, and from that they receive a certain affirmation, and thereby they are strengthened in basic trust. The second thing of importance is that they get an opportunity in their social contacts to express the negative feelings—disappointment, anger—that they will experience in their grief process. Expressing such feelings in this way makes it possible to work them through. Group conversations with aged people can have value for their mental health.

In general it can be said that social contacts increase the awareness of reality; daydreams, illusions, and self-pity have less of a chance to form. One lives in a more emotionally healthy way.

The body plays a special role in all this. We still have no clear picture of the meaning of the body for the aging person, even though medical interest in the process of aging is very great.

A number of aspects of this are visible. First, the body is going to "report" to us more often and more clearly, particularly in a negative way. Disturbances can show themselves in every organ and will have to be reported regularly to the doctor and taken care of. This can be a continuing source of irritation and often of insecurity and anxiety. Second, we have to learn that we can do less and less and that we shall have to accept more and more noticeable limits. This brings its own problems: one must make changes and learn to compensate for what is missing or what does not work right; and one may have to resign oneself to changes, which may bring depression with it.

Many other changes take place in the body in connection with the aging process. One lives less and less energetically; sexual energy diminishes noticeably. One may experience this diminishing of energy and vitality almost as a kind of death; it happens just as it does with plants, beginning at the outer edge and working its way toward the center. One may also experience a slowing of tempo; one needs to stop for rest more often. The range of our activities becomes smaller; we take on less and experience less. So we can say that in the modifications in our bodies we are "helped" in our growth; we become more in touch with our departure. It is a process which is just the reverse of processes in youth. *Then* the changes in our bodies—more vitality, more need for variation, awakening of sexual vitality—helped us in our growth toward adulthood and toward our entry into society, toward living in general.

Human beings live as a psycho-physical unity, a unity of body and spirit. What we experience in our bodies we work out in our spirits. Both body and spirit know the need for rest, for less movement, as the end of life approaches. One may wonder if this is what Freud called a death instinct, a longing of everything that lives to return to the source, to the rest of those not yet born, and thus to death.

The Role of Religion

We have already indicated that two types of religion must be distinguished: one more defensive and the other more dynamic. The faith of a person can have a stagnating function, limiting a person's growth, or it can have the function of supporting growth.

Munnichs writes that, for the accepting of finitude, occupation and confrontation are not enough. "Being able to attribute meaning to finitude can be a first step toward acceptance. The notion that this attribution of meaning is often a response to a call from the far side of death is outside the reach of empirical science. . . . What we are engaged in is working out the connection between meaning and one's life view." As I have indicated, I have some difficulty with this statement by Munnichs. He makes, first of all, an equation between religion and one's life view, and, in doing so, mistakenly ties religion too closely to the concept of attribution of meaning. Even when one gives these words a very vague content (as often happens nowadays), one tends to overlook the realities of religion. I am, moreover, not happy with the phrase, "a call from the far side of death." It is both psychologically and theologically questionable. Neither as a theologian nor as a psychologist have I ever been able to think in terms of such a call. On the contrary, both in theology and in psychology people have always been very critical of such claims. But Munnichs especially overlooks the important question how (religious) attribution of meaning and view of life function in our psychic lives. Specifically, they can function to bring about neurosis, not least among old people. The best example of the positive role of religion for me is the one which we find in the last pages of Han Fortmann's *Oosterse Renaissance,* a fragment that I have mentioned earlier. His words, "the person who has once met God no longer finds the question of a hereafter interesting" clearly sum up his view of the role of religion in relation to finitude. Religious faith is for him a trust which includes the present and the future; it is thus a genuine basic trust and has no further need for theories about the hereafter. It is also my pastoral experience that thoughts about the hereafter play, in general, no great role among old people.

Perhaps we may sum it up this way: a mature and healthy faith makes a contribution to the maturity and integrity of the aging person, but at the same time maturity makes a contribution to the quality of the person's religious life.

This leads us finally to the question of the extent to which an aging person achieves or can achieve such maturity, or whether and to what extent unfinished business from the past plays a part. From developmental psychology we know how the life cycle with its unfinished business can influence a person in the various phases of his existence. It is clear that old people cannot be seen apart from their life cycle, either in their basic personalities or in their reactions to situations. Many aging persons are still beset with developmental difficulties; they may suffer from neuroses; they can be troublesomely passive, dependent, anxious, or aggressive.

In a 1964 publication psychiatrist L. A. Cahn discusses psychiatric problems of old age. It is a good book, which investigates in particular serious mental illness in old age; anyone who deals with old people can, to be sure, get something from it, but it is not entirely relevant for our investigation. What *is* relevant is what he writes about depression and suicide attempts among old people, both of which occur frequently. His studies show that the influence of social factors, and specifically of isolation, is of great importance. From his summing up at the end of the book, here are some striking sentences: "Men, much more than women, are in old age the victims of unfortunate circumstances. . . . The psychological traumas which we found all have as their background the threat of isolation or sickness. . . . Only for a few patients is the loss of one's work situation a serious trauma. For the most part, the consequences of that were financial. . . . *Very likely living alone signifies for the old person a greater stress situation* [italics Cahn's]. . . . In terms of depression, psychological or characterological wounds play a greater part for men than for women. . . . Of the 107 cases studied, 81 suicide attempts were recorded as reactions to particular life circumstances . . . *socially occasioned problems seemed of strikingly heavy weight among male patients as causes of suicide attempts*" [italics Cahn's]. He adds that "an expansion of our knowledge about aging and old age is urgently necessary."[7] I find this observation still completely valid. Specifically, we know very little about the neurotic complications of aging, about which Cahn says less. Research into the consequences of unfinished business in the last phase of life, with reference to the completion of the tasks of the grief process, is very necessary. What are the difficulties, for example, for those who must use denial of finitude?

We also have little experience, so far as I can tell, with psychotherapy for aged people. A number of therapists are of the opinion that old people are too old for therapy. My own judgment is that group conversations for aging people can be of great help and that in a number of cases personal conversation of a counseling sort can bear fruit. I believe that here lies an important work area for trained pastors.

Conclusion

Erikson shows in his studies of puberty and adolescence that society permits the adolescent in most cases a moratorium, a time to get in touch with oneself, a space where, with the understanding and support of others, the adolescent can work out an identity. I would like to plead for a similar time and space for older people at the beginning of the last phase of life, in which they can find their new identities as old people.

To me, such a moratorium would mean:

a. That society would not shove a person into the status of retired person overnight, but would let a person grow more or less gradually toward it, in business life, for example, by a gradual reduction of tasks paired with preparation for the person's new life

b. That society would show just as much respect toward the old person as it does toward the future adult

c. That society would give an opportunity for renewed engagement

d. That society would provide the security of an existence free of financial worries, and of satisfying housing.

We need say little about the purpose of such a moratorium; simply put, it has to support human beings in the finding and keeping of a meaningful place in the community.

8

A View of Aging: Some Theoretical Observations

In the previous chapter we have more or less charted the world of the aging person. Now we want to try to come to a more inclusive view of aging. If one wishes, one can think in terms of a theory of old age. What is aging? We shall try to answer that question by pulling the various elements of old age into an understandable whole.

One could call Munnichs' observations on old age, with their accent on such themes as disengagement, finitude, and renewed engagement, an attempt at such an inclusive theory. One could also call Erikson's view that the aging person must come to a sense of integrity as over against disgust and despair a theory of old age, even though one would have to note that he tries even less than Munnichs to bring together as many elements as possible into such a theory.

A Grief Process

In terms of aging we can distinguish two processes:

a. A physical process: the body grows weaker, one

cannot do as much as one once could; one strikes one's sails and finally ends with death.

b. A psychic process in which various elements may be distinguished:

1. A reaction to the physical process: one must deal with the striking of sails, work it through, and accept it.
2. A weakening of psychic function determined by the bodily changes (such as loss of memory) and the psychic reaction to that. Many people have difficulties with the disappearance of their mental powers.
3. A reaction to a number of external factors important for old people, such as retirement, entry into a home, death of a spouse, isolation.
4. An attempt to influence the physical process in positive ways, such as regular exercise or work: things that we know keep the body healthy.

What is also important for the aging person is the way in which the society regards him, moves him into the category of older person, and so gives him an identity. All aging persons are in a more or less clear way confronted with their bodies and with the image that society has of them. Aging is also to a large extent determined by the way in which they react to this double confrontation and work it through in their lives.

In both confrontations they receive, as it were, the same message: life, you are ready to leave us, or, to use Dante's words, it is time to strike sail. This message is the essence of the experience of finitude, which plays such a central part in the thought of Munnichs.

How does the older person react to this message?

With disengagement, says Munnichs. He lays emphasis on externally perceptible behavior. The nature of any psychic reaction caused or colored by the disengagement remains unclear in his work, although he offers some clues about it. We can trace behind this disengagement a kind of preparatory grief process, and it probably goes through phases.

Munnichs does not discuss that, but it is worth the trouble to do some investigation into the experience of finitude along the same lines, to see if we can discern some phases within the aging process. From the work of Elisabeth Kübler-Ross we are familiar with the phases of denial, anger, bargaining, depression, and acceptance. We have already quoted the Amsterdam psychiatrist Wijngaarden, talking about his own aging process, to the effect that he recognized the anger within himself. We can find similar "signals" among old people, such as grumbling, angry talking, being cynical and negative, all of which point to an anger not yet dealt with and a dissatisfaction with one's lot. It would be worth the trouble to pursue the question when and whether these signs disappear, in order to see if they constitute, or are connected with, a particular phase of aging. One must also realize that among aging persons there can be, and often is, a notion that the process through which they are going is unavoidable, a given part of life.

We notice that among aging people there is also a resignation, which can turn into a longing to die. I have already indicated Freud's concept of a death instinct. In his book, *Beyond the Pleasure Principle,* he suggests that in all living things there is, alongside the principle of the continuation and expansion of life (symbolized by Eros), a longing to return to the condition of the beginning, of non-being, of death. He even thinks—although he says that his observations are quite speculative—that this tendency toward death is perhaps the most fundamental force at work in living things. If that is true, then that kind of tendency is bound to be expressed in mental or emotional phenomena. Well, we know in human psychic life that next to an anxiety about death (which is biologically useful and necessary in order to keep human life going), there is a deeply rooted longing for death, especially for the rest which death brings. In an article I have already mentioned, "Death in Human Experience," I have indicated this double experience of the mystery of death, and have tried to suggest, with all kinds of examples, how real this longing is. The imagery of earth's bosom, of the eternal home, suggests it. Is it not conceivable that in aging, as the anxiety about death diminishes (and, from a biological point of view, is no longer so necessary), this longing becomes the major voice? Even the quicker readiness to consider suicide, which we can note in older people, can be a manifestation of this. This applies to the more general need for rest, which we have already mentioned.

We must now ask, What about the "renewed engagement" Munnichs talks about? Is it not in direct opposition to what we have just said?

A curious paradox is revealed here, but it is a paradox for which there are parallels elsewhere. The Dutch poet Jacqueline van der Waals writes, in a poem called "Now That I Know," that she experiences life far more intensely "now that she knows" she is going to die. Perhaps we can talk about this more clearly.

We have already spoken of an anticipated leave-taking and of preparatory grief work in aging. A parallel which throws light on this problem can be found in the collection *Death and Identity,* in an essay entitled "Observations Concerning Fear of Death in Fatally Ill Children and Their Mothers."[1] It is a report on research done in an American hospital, in which mothers, after they were told that their children were seriously ill and had but a few months to live, were given the opportunity to care for their children in the hospital alongside the nurses. They also had regular contact with physicians, who kept them carefully informed about the course of the disease and its treatment. Other staff members in the hospital also worked regularly with the mothers.

What seemed to happen was that, generally speaking, the mothers went through three phases which took about four months. The first phase was one of *denial*, not wanting to admit the truth. This was followed by a phase of *realistic approach*, in which on the one hand the mother did her best to prolong the child's life as much as possible, but on the other hand gradually gave up hope and tried to help her child more realistically. In this phase a kind of emotional detachment became visible. Finally, there was a third phase, marked by *acceptance*, in which wishes that the child would be released from its pain could be expressed. For some mothers in this phase there was even a kind of sublimation; they went about helping other mothers. The curious thing was that near the end hospital staff members often had more difficulty accepting the death of the child than the mothers did.

In the second phase involving realistic approach there is on the one hand a certain hope but on the other hand a clear reckoning with the process of the illness; along with an interest in treatment there developed an interest in the emotional needs of the child in its illness. This kind of turning toward the child can be compared, perhaps, with the "renewed engagement" of Munnichs. In this renewed engagement one can speak of a genuine involvement with a piece of work, a hobby, something one can actually do, just as the mother can deal realistically with the child, bathing, feeding, and filling the child's day in a practical way. But one can also speak of a certain distance, feeling oneself attached to things in a way that is emotionally different from what it was before. It remains a hobby; the older person dealing with the finitude of existence approaches reality differently. Here, too, there is a parallel to the mother's dealing with the sick child. As the mother becomes involved with medical treatment, gets interested in it (and in the illness itself), it means that between mother and child a kind of distance arises, a feeling of being emotionally tied to the child in a different way, coming to terms with finitude and a loosening of the bonds. This enables the mother to ask what the child's emotional needs are because of the sickness. The emotional process goes on on two levels. At a deep level there is a "knowledge of finitude," of having to let go; but on the surface, on a more visible level a turning toward the child, sometimes with great intensity. These two influence and support each other. It is the same process that we see in the poem of Jacqueline van der Waals, who, "now that she knows," becomes tied to things and people in a more intense way. This double process is a preparation for acceptance; in the exact sense of the phrase it is a process of preparatory grief.

In this process certain anxieties can arise just as they did with the mothers of the sick children. For example, we often hear old people say that they are afraid of becoming childish and thus burdens to those around them. For many people, even if anxiety about death itself gradually disappears, the fear of having cancer or of having to undergo a painful process of dying plays a large part. And many people can be trapped in the fear that they will lose their minds or have a dehumanizing illness. Simone de Beauvoir offers examples of this.

Still other parallels between the process taking place with the mothers and the grief process of aging can be found. Research on aging suggests more and more often that among old people there is a visible need to evaluate their lives. If we try to put ourselves in the mothers' place, we can easily imagine that in the long process of caring for the child the thought arises, What has this child, perhaps in a way different from other children, meant for me and for our family? One sums up life, so to speak, in this way, and finds oneself on the way to departure. In the conversations with old people reported by P. Brouns in an unpublished dissertation, he found the evaluation of one's own life to be a hallmark of early old age. He writes: "Looking back is always a part of a more general process of letting go. Looking back and making judgments involves a certain taking of distance."[2] Here he is in agreement with such writers as Charlotte Bühler.[3]

The purpose of such an evaluation is to come to a judgment about oneself. The old person asks, "What have I done with it?" With reference to oneself, judgment and rounding off go together. Here Erikson's concept of integrity comes into its own, with its opposite poles of disgust and despair, which come into play when there is no more time to round life off in a more satisfying manner. There is a story about a German professor who had devoted his whole life to the study of the Greek word fragment *hypo-* and who came to the realization on his deathbed that he really should have studied the word *apo-*. In its ridiculousness this story lays bare deeply anchored human structures. We have already spoken of the need to be able to accept oneself and to be accepted by others. In such a story these needs are assumed, and they are things that (as we have seen) also come into play in the religious concept of a last divine judgment, present in many religions.

In the grief process of aging we come in the third place ever more clearly to a confrontation with death; first with finitude, as Munnichs describes things, but later with death as an approaching reality. The increasing confrontation with death of people one knows in the vicinity around one plays a large part in this.[4] Death remains for us human beings a mystery, something rather bigger than a riddle to be solved. We can express our attitude of fear or trust in the face of this mystery only by means of symbols that stand for the fear or the trust. We speak of the jaws of death or of death as a return to mother's bosom. In many usages surrounding death we have given a certain solidity to these attitudes and symbols. They help us, more or less, to live with death.

On closer examination these symbols do not seem accidental. They refer to a religiousness living deep in human beings or to a faith created during their lives: two great things that can be distinguished from each other, but which in concrete instances seem to be connected. We can recognize this religiousness in the customs and symbols having to do with death. But we have as yet given little study to the problems connected with it. And so what I am talking about here remains tentative and incompletely founded. What we see at deaths and burials is that the family gathers for them almost instinctively. The idea apparently remains in us that death has something to do with the connectedness and continuation of the generations in history.

It is as if we think that at death something is transferred and continued; it is precisely at the time of a death that we feel that in our depths something binds us together as human beings. My former teacher, Dr. H. T. de Graaf, was fond of speaking of an inexhaustible connectedness of life held on to and honored in religion. He himself formulated the religious attitude toward death in these words: "God is the Lord of death." Even through death the inexhaustible connectedness of life is continued. This is a general religious attitude toward death, which different people express in different ways. We are dealing again with basic trust, which catches death up in a greater and more fundamental connection. This religious image does not *need* to lead to thoughts of human immortality, but there is no question that it has often done so. We are more in the neighborhood of what Munnichs calls the attribution of meaning to finitude.

Next to this religious vision we must suggest another which is better referred to as the vision of faith. Especially in the Protestant sectors of Christendom, the relationship between human beings and God is experienced as one between two persons, in which God, as Creator of human beings and the world has a particular claim upon us which we, however, do not always honor. We "fall away" from God and in so doing become prey to the power of death, which rules this world, a power which is the enemy of both God and human beings. Through our belief in a loving God coming to us in Christ we are freed from the power of death and can rise from the dead. In this line of thought resurrection stands over against immortality, and faith over against religion. What is psychologically true of both is basic trust, which is primarily related to the appearance of Christ and puts us in a position to stand over against death with trust. One can say that, in both cases, God as the life which transcends death and which binds us together across the generations is the central thought from the psychological perspective. If this be true, then the discussion about projection, which is of great significance for the position of Christian faith in the modern world (and which awaits deeper treatment) can move into new areas. Unfortunately, we must at this point stop with this indication.

From this viewpoint, what light is cast upon the concept of integrity so important for Erikson? This concept appears to represent a combination of various elements. Erikson himself says that he can give no definitive definition. But we seem to encounter the following elements in it. First, there is the accent on evaluation. This is a means whereby human beings are caught up in the process of letting go. Second is the accent on the acceptance of one's given life cycle. We have seen that the need to come to terms with this life cycle plays a part here. Finally, it involves the inner readiness to put oneself no longer at the center of life. On the contrary, the readiness to back off and to make the way free for others is an important element in a successful old age. Integrity means that the aging person ends life in such a way that a new beginning connected with it would be possible. It may be that one finds a place in the inexhaustible connectedness of life but also that one believes oneself able to continue living his life with God, and finally that one may be reborn in another incarnation.

A few remarks to close this part of the chapter. As we have said, one can see the "growth" in old age as a sort of grief process in which one lets go of life with one's fellow human beings, one's work, one's interests, without the opportunity of investing one's libido anew in other objects. Those who have made a clear representation (or image) of living in an afterlife form an exception to this, but we have several times noticed in this book that a clear commitment to an afterlife—barring a few exceptions such as Paul—seldom occurs. People apparently experience death mostly as non-being. Even when one is a person of faith one may remain agnostic about representations (or images) of life after death, so that a transfer of libidinous attachment to this life over to an attachment to a life to come seldom appears.

Libido is to a great extent directed toward oneself. We deal with our own needs: our hobbies, our own problems, our children and grandchildren. We allow ourselves this luxury after a life loaded with work. Alongside this stands a need for rest, as we have seen; Freud has some essential things to say about this. So human beings experience an aging process fed from two deep springs. There is on the one hand a need for rest, to pull oneself out of the world and back into oneself, and there is on the other hand a need to participate in life and activity but in a more distanced way, not with a passion for performance. In the ongoing process of aging the accent on the mixing of both needs gradually shifts.

With regard to experiencing death we must make some final remarks. Experience teaches that the acceptance of death grows with the advance of the years, at least for the majority of people. We must not, however, draw from this the conclusion that no negative reactions intrude in cases of acute danger of death. At such points even older people who otherwise impress us as mature may display immature reactions, if one may use that term. In everyone's life there is a quantity of unfinished business, which can manifest itself under such circumstances. Aging is a process of growing toward more acceptance and more relinquishing, but in the depths of oneself no one arrives completely at the endpoint of that process and there is always some stagnation.

Theoretical Considerations

We have seen that aging is in reality a kind of grief process, a learning to let go, or, as Munnichs calls it, an "anticipated leave-taking." The element of learning is present in it; the letting go comes in bits and pieces. First comes retirement, then problems with one's health, after that the loss of friends and family members, and finally the definitive leave-taking.

All this stands at the same time under the influence of nature, of developments in our bodies, the organic underpinnings of our existence. This influence is in a certain sense a help in the aging process. One can view aging as a pulling back of vitality in the organism and thereby in one's whole existence. Plants wilt; they grow limp; their leaves change color and fall off. A comparable process also takes place in us, one which we may call a dismantling, though the word is not very lovely. This bodily "wilting" probably has an influence on our psychic vitality: the need to limit the dimensions of our living, of which Bühler speaks, the slower tempo that we gradually develop, the growing need for rest, are all phenomena which are included in this "wilting." Alongside this are the diminishing of sensory functions (we can't see or hear as well), the increased inability of our motor system to be at our disposal, and the diminishing of our sexuality. They lead almost unnoticeably to an acceptance of the developmental task of this phase of life, just as happens (in reverse) in growth toward adolescence and adulthood. I would also place the diminishing of anxiety about death in this category; it is another part of "wilting," as there exists no vital necessity to ward off death.

We therefore have to do with a process operating on two levels. On the surface we see a grief process, with phases in which one goes through anger, powerlessness, and depression toward acceptance, a process in which anxiety often plays a large part, sometimes made sharper by a great deal of isolation. What the psychiatrist Terruwe reminds us—that to be able to live well a person requires the affirmation of others—certainly holds true for old people: they need the confirmation of regular social contact with others. On the deeper level we can trace a process which through resignation and acceptance comes to a waiting for death, even a looking forward to it.

We have seen the youth of human beings as a learning period in which they go through development in a series of phases. It was especially Erikson who tried to show that in this development three patterns are visible next to each other, continually influencing each other. Development consists of three aspects: physical, social, and psychic. In this book all three aspects are dealt with, and to a large extent so is their connectedness. We have indicated the connection between physical and psychic development in the preceding pages. Is there also a connection that we can demonstrate between these personal aspects and the social aspects of aging?

We have seen that there are certain influences of social patterns on the personal life of aging persons. There is a clear influence of release or retirement on the psyche, even though the consequences of that have not been fully researched. Formally joining the ranks of "senior citizens," with the over-sixty-five passes and other privileges that may ensue, must also have a psychological effect. Then there are such things as housing and medical care, and the whole business of getting information, in all of which the society engages itself, sometimes quite deeply, with the lives of older people. But we may not say that there is a clearly structured pattern operating out of clear concepts, which supports development in this later phase. In youth it is quite different, and much better. Society is obviously interested in the way in which the growing adolescent will later take his place, and therefore arranges a well-ordered process of preparation, growth, and adaptation. Socialization plays a great part, even during the early years of education. In many European countries, and to a lesser extent in America, a number of different types of schools are made available to young people, and in some communities society guides and supports their development through specialized medical advice. In the young person, society sees its future ahead of it and makes itself responsible in particular ways. The society provides old people with plenty of "care," but there appears to be little sense of connectedness and responsibility for them.

Another question arises behind this one. In youth, development obviously occurs in phases. Is there in the aging years a similar development to be seen, and is it conceivable that there are parallels between the development of young people and that of old people, though perhaps in the opposite direction? If Erikson is right about development in young people, this could mean that in old age there are also three distinguishable aspects which mutually influence each other. The interested reader will understand that research about development in old people is still taking its first steps, as compared with young people's development, so that we cannot go farther than expressing some suppositions. But let us at least try to formulate a few observations.

I was put on the trail of this kind of question by some remarks in the study by A. Polspoel entitled *Crying over the*

Lost Ego.[5] The author analyzes the grief process, and, in so doing, suggests that in this process there is a regression of the ego to earlier phases of development. The griever gives evidence, for example, of a need for dependency and security, and behaves (more or less) childishly. Grieving thus includes an identity process, in which the griever goes "down" or "back" to an earlier stage of development, and then returns. In the grief process among older people the upward movement has a certain character. In a normal grief process the development goes in the direction of freedom to make new attachments to others, and thus to renew the fabric of living. But letting go of life itself in the confrontation with finitude gives no opportunity to move toward new connections. The freedom which people build here is the freedom to become oneself in a deeper sense, to accept finitude and to reengage oneself in a more detached way.

And what happens in the "downward" movement? Are there indications that aging people, although perhaps in a changed sequence, face the same problems they met in their younger years as they grew toward adulthood? And can we recognize in such a process the same phases? I propose as a hypothesis for further research that this is precisely the case. Let me make clear what I mean.

a. Let us begin with puberty. This is the time when a young person makes the first steps from childhood to adulthood, and works for the first time at developing an identity. The phase of childhood is definitely closed off. The young person seeks connections with peer groups in order to discover this new identity. Sexuality is clearly involved in one way or another, and erotic feelings make new and deeper relationships with other people possible. There is still considerable freedom, but one's responsibilities in society announce themselves. One can, I think, compare this phase with the period of sixty to sixty-five years of age.

By means of retirement and pension, there is an obvious shift. Here begins the loss of a social identity.

One is a *former* teacher, a *former* policeman. Through this loss, this first confrontation with finitude, one becomes open to the concept of becoming and being old. The pressure which society exercises, in the form of a number of demands, diminishes. There is less that one "has" to do, and one reaches a stage in which a feeling of freedom dominates life. Sexuality diminishes, and the need for contact with peer groups increases. In this phase, as in the corresponding one of youth, one begins to seek and to experience one's new identity. Among old people erotic feelings are still alive, but in contrast to puberty these feelings do not serve the purpose of discovering deeper relationships, but of holding on to a particular intimacy, which gradually diminishes with aging.

The parallels between the two phases strike me as obvious. In the two shifts, the younger person and the older one are going in opposite directions. But there are phenomena which point to a kinship between the two on a deeper level.

b. Before the phase of puberty come the school years, in which the problem is the development of a sense of industry, and the oedipal years, somewhere between four and eight, when the problem is one of developing initiative. If we keep in mind that it is true for aging people that society and its demands are growing vaguer, while young people are preparing themselves for life in society, and are thus feeling its demands on them, then we discover obvious parallels in "industry," being industriously busy at school and the hobbies of the retired person. There are many jobs, including leadership in a number of organizations, that one gladly and industriously performs now that there are no more demands piling up. Older people are often very busy people. And in the voluntary performance of tasks we can see a parallel with the oedipal period. More than before, the older person does more things out of himself, because they are visible to him and he gets from them a feeling that he still counts for something, a feeling that is also an important aspect of the oedipal period.

c. Now we come to the earliest phases of childhood years and the last phase of aging. In the third and fourth years of life (called by some developmental psychologists the anal phase) the central mark, according to Erikson, is the early triumph of an uncertain autonomy: the child begins to walk, take care of itself, and possibly resists the surrounding world in a childishly stubborn way. What is striking about many aging people is their fear of becoming dependent. They resist admission to an old people's home as long as possible, because "that's the end of your freedom." The maintenance of self-reliance, especially in relation to the helping environment, is for most old people, especially in the last phase of old age, a deep need. Here is a clear parallel to the second phase of children's development.

d. The first phase of development, the so-called oral phase, is the one in which the child is completely cared for and in which basic trust develops. This phase involves a motherly surrounding, a warmth like that of the nest, which apparently has a deeply formative influence. The correspondence to the last phase of old age is clear: when the old person realizes and accepts the fact that he can no longer care for himself, and so must give up his autonomy—however gradually—he becomes ready to let himself be cared for. What he needs, and intuitively gets, is "the warmth of the nest," a caring, motherly surrounding. Here what is required is a respect which knows how to avoid infantilization in dealing with old people, and from which warmth, patience, and rest are not excluded. It is an atmosphere in which the old person can relax and so can experience a firm ground under his existence, which can lead to a basic trust in this ending phase. We have already seen how important such basic trust is for a good attitude toward death.

In this phase death is not only no longer feared, but is expected and sometimes even wished for. The expression often used is typical of this phase; one hears old people say that now they have "seen it all." Seeing is one of the very first things that a child can do. Perception begins with seeing. Apparently, the accent falls on seeing once again in this last phase.

e. If it is true that aging is a walking through the phases of childhood in reverse, this casts a special light on dying. Dying then becomes a return to the source, a return to mother's womb. There is a full set of indications, from which it appears—perhaps not consciously but certainly in deeper levels of the personality—that people look forward to death as such a return. Hall talks explicitly about a return to the womb. Before he died, Francis of Assisi said that he wanted to do it "in the arms of Lady Poverty," and stretched himself out naked on the ground. The return to the source, to mother, is visible in this statement. The customs at death, as well, such as burial and cremation, indicate that this is how it is experienced throughout the world. At burials we often speak of entrusting someone to the bosom of the earth; cremation, too, has in religious history the meaning of being united with the powers of the source of life. The need of family members to come together at deaths and funerals points to an unconscious need to experience, precisely at these moments, something of the bosom of the family, tying source and end together.

On the basis of these indications we can posit a correspondence between development in childhood and that of the aging process. Development in childhood moves in the direction of the realization of possibilities; human beings are active, even aggressive, in this period. An upward-moving, expansive power is stored up in them, the kind of thing sometimes called a vital force. In the phases in which such development takes place there is an obvious correlation with needs and tasks coming from society. In aging there is a development in the opposite direction; we see a "wilting" of possibilities; one is no longer so active, one can even be called passive, one lets things go. We can speak of a pulling back of the vital force: older people limit their activities; they complain about no longer being able to do things as well; they are tired out. In the phases of this development the correlation with expectations from the society breaks down, and the older person does not see himself as a participant in his life, his culture. We can indeed talk, as Dante does, of "striking sails." After a completed voyage, one sails into safe harbor.

One final question, a question not often asked in modern psychology, but which is useful for our view of aging and for our dealings with aged people. Can one distinguish types of old people?

Probably so. In the first place, one thinks of the type of old person who at retirement experiences a clear break in existence, as over against another type for whom continuity is dominant: artists, politicians, housewives. For increasing numbers of people in our society the important problem of the shift to another life pattern begins at retirement. Business employees, workers, civil servants, for example, must often work their way through an obvious period of adjustment. Relatively little study has been made of the problems attached to this adjustment. The superficial research that has been done makes it appear that at the beginning these problems are experienced as demanding, but that within a period of one or two years the adjustment has been made.

We can also distinguish between the old people for whom aging, and all that it brings, represents a fulfillment of needs, sometimes childish ones, and those who have difficulties with that. The first group is happy to become dependent and to experience security or perhaps to build into their lives some freedom and independence which they could not find in their jobs and that they now happily experience in retirement. The second type has difficulty with certain aspects of aging, often because of another kind of infantile need; they miss the affirmation that work brought with it, the contact with people; they live out of a need to be needed; they also miss the confirmation that lies hidden in daily work, and now they feel uncertain. Sometimes they even miss a certain independence that work brought with it.

Among old people we can also distinguish between those who are anxious and isolated and those who are occupied and happy or, from another viewpoint, between those who are embittered and rancorous and those who are tolerant, loving, and mature; finally, one can distinguish between those who are defensive and closed up and those who are open and active.

Faith plays, as we have seen, an important role in all this. Not in the sense that some people suppose, that believers are more occupied and happy, but rather that faith can help build in maturity and openness, but can also contribute to the entrenchment of a defensive, closed attitude. The role of faith depends on how it is used.

9

Pastoral Work with Old People

What is pastoral work?

Before we try to answer that question, some preliminary observations. In the first place, the answer depends on the area in which the pastor works. He can be a pastor in a congregation or a parish and within this setting work with old people. He can also be employed in a home as a specialist exclusively concerned with the interests and problems of old people. He may—although this is far more likely in the Netherlands than in America—work in a welfare agency and exercise his role as pastor within that setting; in that case he will work as a team member with physicians, social workers, and other specialists. In general one can say that, whatever the nature of the setting in which he works, he will have three fixed points which more or less determine his work. In the first place he is concerned with people; he feels himself responsible in a particular way for people and for the quality of their life. Second, he is concerned for the gospel; he draws his work among people from the work and message of Jesus Christ, in which he ever more deeply steeps himself. His third takeoff point is the church, in whose service he stands; it also pays his salary. This church can be a concrete Protestant or Roman Catholic judicatory of which he is an "official," and which has educated him and taken him into its service, but it can also be the Church, with the capital letter symbolizing the great fellowship of believers embracing all church organizations, which forms the background against which he sees his work, even if he is paid by a home or an agency.

The second preliminary remark is, as we said in chapter 2, that the character of pastoral work is strongly determined by the fact that we live in a shift from an agrarian to a metropolitan and industrial society. The consequence of this is that in the pastorate the accents lie on the authority that he possesses as pastor much less than they once did. There is also less emphasis on maintenance of morality or on the proclamation for which he is particularly responsible. In an urban society the accent falls more on being with people in the problems of their existence, on the quality of life, which is threatened and must be defended, and finally on the free, independent judgment of people themselves.

The third remark is that in modern society we no longer think of the pastorate as something set apart, a clerical group attached to an institution, but rather that the pastorate can be, perhaps must be, something that people do for one another and with one another, for example within a group. The arena in which we want to see pastoral work in this chapter is that of a church congregation or parish or a home for the aged. We shall leave aside the question of pastors working in an agency or on a welfare team.

We begin with a view of pastoral work which, I think, is acceptable both to Roman Catholics and to Protestants. I formulate it as follows: pastoral work among old people consists in stimulating them and helping them live and experience their existence in the light of God. I understand the "light of God" to mean the light of the kingdom of God or of the gospel or of the event of Jesus Christ. There is no opposition among these; the message of the kingdom and Jesus Christ belong to each other.

The second question which we must ask is, Who are the old people at whom our pastoral work is aimed?

First, we must say that old people form a special group in society marked by the fact that they are in danger of being isolated and thus alienated from real things, and that this isolation and alienation have consequences. If we wish to get to the point in our pastoral work where old people live their lives in the light of God, then we must be aware of this danger.

Pastoral work with old people must therefore include the following elements:

a. Stimulating old people toward doing things for themselves. Isolation always affects the courage to live, and such courage can only prosper on the basis of the desire to do something ourselves about changing and improving our existence.

b. Improving the structures within which old people live. This involves, for example, finding groups in which people can break through the isolation. It also involves alerting businesses to the problems of preparation for retirement. The cooperation of physicians and social workers is important for this task.

c. Engaging oneself as a pastor with the problems of aging. Seeking old people out, listening to them, thinking with them. These elements recall what we read about Jesus Christ in the Gospels, specifically about his attitude toward groups which were isolated in his time and who were alienated from essential things: the poor, the publicans, the women. We read how he sought them out, listened to them, thought with them, shared meals with them. In this way he pointed to the coming kingdom, already present in his work. Thus he made these people feel that they, too, belonged: to people, to society, to God and the future. He freed these people for a life of their own, a life lived in love, hope, and faith. We need to notice that he left the structures of society untouched. That is not valid, however, for us. We do not exactly know why Jesus and the early Christians (one thinks of Paul's attitude toward slavery) took such an attitude. It is not impossible that among other things the expectation of the quick coming of God's kingdom played a part. I am convinced that at this point we need to go a step farther.

But we must give a second answer to the question we have posed. The old people among whom we work are in the second place the people who have come to a particular phase in their life cycles, and who therefore face new demands and new possibilities. Different descriptions of this last are given in the literature. We have seen that some speak of a confrontation with finitude and of learning to accept that. We have described the task as a grief process in which the problem of having to let go plays a large part. Erikson sees the tension of these years consisting in the struggle for integrity as over against giving in to despair. As we looked at pastoral work, I described the task and possibility of aging as having to (and being able to) end our lives in God's light.

What light is cast by this task on the content and method of pastoral work among old people?

In the first place, the task, as I see it, does *not* consist in "announcing" these tasks and possibilities. We have learned to see that preaching is an essential element in pastoral work, but that the almost exclusive emphasis which people have often placed on proclamation has led, as one psychiatrist expressed it in a meeting with pastors, to firing off projectiles without knowing whether they were well aimed and would hit their targets. Proclamation, we have discovered, is only possible on the basis of solidarity, of going to stand where the other person stands, as Christ worked and spoke in his day out of a solidarity with those who were then discriminated against. Pastoral work thus begins with listening and with empathy. There must be a rapport, a closeness, which at the same time includes a certain amount of distance. On this basis, the pastor tries to walk with the other person, and in the process within each one and in their relationship, there comes a need for what one may call proclamation, a word of faith from the pastor. But the way to that word may be long, and the pastor must listen well in order to know what "word of faith" is needed here. Listening means that one comes to a sort of clarity in which the depth of faith becomes visible, in which the word can apply and function. Often there is in the Gospels mention of "seeing through" the other, a view *of* and *in* the other person in his relationship to himself and to God. I think that this is what Paul Pruyser is talking about when he refers to pastoral diagnosis. The word of the pastor or pastoral worker can help the other person in his struggle to come to integrity and faith. But it can only reach the other person when it is not a missile shot from a distance, but when it, in solidarity and in a feeling of being understood, *touches* the other person. This includes the necessity that the pastor doubts and seeks along with the other person, and, as it were, *lives* his faithful proclamation. The faith he proclaims must, in a manner of speaking, always be acquainted with the despair and disgust, not just in the other person, but in himself.

There is yet a third aspect to the answer. The old people to whom our ministry is directed are also *fellow-believers* with the pastor, even when they are perhaps doubting or negative. By this I intend to convey the fact that the pastor must see old people as those who, along with him, belong to the church. (Here we may understand church as a particular congregation to stand for the great fellowship of believers.) That is to say, the pastor sees them as standing in the light of God and sharing in the mystery of the religious community.

This is true even when they themselves may react negatively to such thoughts. And thus he feels himself connected to them through his pastoral responsibility. This involves seeing them as together—together with us—on the road to God's future, to the kingdom, to salvation, and that we therefore come to them out of the background of being gathered before God, out of the background of what in theological terms is called a cultic gathering. That is to say, we bring in our contacts with them the "flavor" of the eucharist or of the sermon, and our concern for them means a (sometimes unexpressed but often openly acknowledged) invitation to celebrate with us the deepest secret of life and death.

So we always do our work as pastors among old people also as ministers of the rites and as proclaimers of Christ, both in the congregation at worship as well as in the more personal relationship of home visits and calls on the sick. What binds us together and is the concern for which we have special responsibility is the belief in God's future, which lights the house of the old as well as the young like a candle in the darkness. Many pastors will want to talk explicitly about faith in the resurrection; for me the belief in God's future is the essential thing of this faith.

I believe that there are certain dangers in the pastorate with old people which are not always recognized and which deserve consideration. Let me name a few which are, in my view, important:

a. The danger that we as pastors see older people as already on their way to death, already dying. In reality this means doing what our society so often does, namely "writing them off." Older people no longer really belong; they live in separate houses or neighborhoods and must be seen and dealt with by the pastor as a separate category. I would plead for a view in which old people are seen as people in the middle of our society who experience its problems in an acute way and who could make a contribution of their own to reflection on the developments of our society. They live in the present, but are negotiating a particular phase of their lives, just as every person is negotiating a phase of life. This means that they have special problems to solve, which often keep them intensely busy and sometimes make them into very aware and vital (at least psychically vital) people.

b. The danger, that we also share with others in our society, of tending to regard older people as powerless, indeed as "under age." Using nicknames such as "Pop" or "Mom" betrays something of that attitude. We are glad to care for others, and of course for older people, but the amount of power we are exercising and the lack of respect we have for them may get hidden.

c. The danger which lies in the tendency of many people, and therefore also of pastors, of being too directive with older people. We sit there full of advice and so-called experience, holding stereotyped views of older people as living outside full life and having small horizons. Those stereotypes quickly bring us to a point where we are all too ready to take away some of their freedom and their need to experience their own lives by putting our directives between them and life.

d. Finally, there creeps in almost unnoticed in our pastoral work a tendency to see our pastoral responsibility as a preparation for the end, or as helping people in their weakness, or often as giving advice on the conduct of life. Whoever sees his fellows, even older people, with the eyes of Christ and in the light of the kingdom of God, sees people with a particular task and with their own struggles, and will therefore see standing next to them and listening to them and thinking with them as the first and most important task of the pastor.

To end this chapter I want to make some remarks about the cooperation of lay people in ministry to older people. There are special possibilities for lay people, and perhaps special tasks. All kinds of things are identified and indicated in what has been said up to now. If it is the task of the pastor to be an enabler, one who brings things to life in the life of a group or a person and thereby makes development and renewal possible, this task can also be transferred to lay people. All the things that go with that—being able to listen, having empathy, bringing such abilities to consciousness, taking people to church, reading aloud from the Gospels—are not tasks for the professional pastor alone. On the contrary, it is the pastorally oriented lay person who may often accomplish this more than the pastor. We must apply ourselves to giving pastoral helpers a better grasp of these tasks than we have heretofore done. I would add that such helping professionals as nurses, aides, and physical therapists can be helped to bring out their own hidden pastoral qualities, and to develop them. We must break up the stereotyped image that pastoral work is the exclusive territory of ordained people.

Alongside the world of the aged there is a great area lying fallow. The sick and the dying, widows and divorced persons, homophiles and migrant workers—all tend to belong to the forgotten groups in our efficiency-oriented society, and all are allowed to lapse into isolation. To do pastoral work means that one helps such persons feel that there is a fellowship to which they belong and that they can know a portion of this fellowship in their strivings to be human. Among many of these groups there is already much work being done by lay people, often by volunteers. Pastoral training for these volunteers would be a major contribution. Are we pastors with our pastoral work not too far out toward the margins of society?

Notes

Chapter 1

1. H. C. Rümke, *Levenstijdperken van de Man* (Amsterdam, 1938). A good English translation of this title would be *Stages of a Man's Life*, which happens to be the title of an American book published many years later.

2. *Ibid.*, pp. 108-10.

3. Simone de Beauvoir, *La Vieillesse* (*De Ouderdom*, Utrecht, 1975). Professor Faber cites, and apparently worked from, the Dutch translation.

4. H. T. de Graaf, *De Godsdienst in het Licht der Zielkunde* (Assen, 1928).

Chapter 2

1. In some ways the shift to an urban, metropolitan society as described by Professor Faber is more visible in the author's own country than in the United States. In, say, 1946, it was important to address a letter to an acquaintance by including one or more "adjectives of respect," something like our "Reverend," before the addressee's name; a letter not so addressed could even be returned

to the sender. That custom has almost completely disappeared in the Netherlands now, though not entirely. American society has not been marked in *recent* years by such shifts in social stratification, but other changes have been equally profound. For example, rural electrification between 1935 and 1950 produced revolutionary changes in rural life *(translator)*.

Chapter 3

1. The author is referring specifically to the situation in the Netherlands at this point. The church in the U.S.A. took similar actions, but somewhat later.

2. H. von Bracken and H. P. David, *Perspektiven der Persönlichkeitstheorie* (Bern-Stuttgart, 1959).

3. Charlotte Bühler, *Der menschliche Lebenslauf als psychologisches Problem* (Leipzig, 1932), 2nd ed. (Göttingen, 1959).

4. J. M. A. Munnichs, *Ouderdom en Eindigheid* (Assen, 1964).

5. Elaine Cumming and W. H. Henry, *Growing Old: The Process of Disengagement* (New York: Basic Books, Publishers, 1961).

6. E. H. Erikson, *Identity and the Life Cycle* (New York: W. W. Norton & Co., 1968).

Chapter 4

1. Margaret Mead, *Culture and Commitment* (Garden City, N.Y.: Natural History Press, 1970).

Chapter 5

1. P. Brouns, *Reflectie op pastoraal Handelen bij Bejaarden*. Unpublished essay, Theological Faculty of Tilburg, The Netherlands.

2. H. Faber, *Profiel van een Bedelaar* (Meppel, 1975). The Dutch title could be translated as *Profile of a Beggar*.

Chapter 7

1. Han M. M. Fortmann, *Oosterse Renaissance*, "Easter Renaissance" (Bilthoven, 1970), p. 67.

2. T. W. Adorno, et al., *The Authoritarian Personality* (New York: John Wiley & Sons, 1964).
3. Gordon W. Allport, *The Nature of Prejudice* (New York: Doubleday & Co., 1958).
4. David O. Moberg, "Religiosity in Old Age," in Bernice Neugarten, ed., *Middle Age and Aging: A Reader in Social Psychology* (University of Chicago Press, 1968).
5. Erikson, *Identity and the Life Cycle,* pp. 139-40.
6. *Ibid.*, p. 141.
7. L. A. Cahn, *Psychiatrische Problemen van de Oude Dag, (Psychiatric Problems of Old Age)* (The Hague, 1964).

Chapter 8

1. Robert Fulton, ed., *Death and Identity* (New York: John Wiley & Sons, 1965).
2. Brouns, *Reflectie op pastoraal Handelen bij Bejaarden.*
3. Cf. Bühler, *Der menschliche Lebenslauf als psychologiches Problem.*
4. Cf. Jan Matse, *Het laatste Kwartier (The Last Quarter),* (Meppel, 1977).
5. A. Polspoel, *Wenen om het verloren Ik (Crying over the Lost Ego),* (Hilversum, 1979).

Bibliography

Works Available in English

Adorno, T. W., et al. *The Authoritarian Personality*. New York: Harper & Brothers, 1950.

Allport, Gordon W. *The Nature of Prejudice*. Westport, Conn.: Greenwood Press, 1965.

Beauvoir, Simone de. *The Coming of Age*. New York: The Putnam Publishing Group, 1972. (orig. French, *La Vieillesse*.)

Carp, Frances M. *Retirement*. New York: Behavioral Publications, 1972.

Cumming, Elaine, and Henry, W. H. *Growing Old: The Process of Disengagement*. New York: Basic Books, Publishers, 1961.

Durkheim, Emile. *The Elementary Forms of the Religious Life*. London: George Allen & Unwin, 1976 (c1915).

Fulton, Robert, ed. *Death and Identity*. New York: John Wiley & Sons, 1965.

Hall, C. Stanley. *Senescence: the Last Half of Life*. New York: D. Appleton & Co., 1922.

Mead, Margaret. *Culture and Commitment*. Garden City, N.Y.: Natural History Press, 1970.

Neugarten, Bernice, ed. *Middle Age and Aging: A Reader in Social Psychology*. University of Chicago Press, 1968.

Works Not Available in English

H. C. I. Andriessen, *Groei en Grens in de Volwassenheid*. Nijmegen, 1970.

P. C. Boutens, *Stemmen*. Amsterdam, 1925.

P. Brouns, *Reflectie op pastoraal Handelen bij Bejaarden*. Unpublished essay. Theologische Faculteit te Tilburg.

Charlotte Bühler, *Der menschliche Lebenslauf als psychologisches Problem*. Leipzig, 1932, 2nd ed., Göttingen, 1959. Although this particular work has not been translated into English, several other works by Bühler in the same general area of interest have been.

L. A. Cahn, *Psychiatrische Problemen van de Oude Dag*. 's-Gravenhage, 1964.

H. Faber, *Profiel van een Bedelaar*. Meppel, 1975.

———, *Over Dood en Sterven*. Leiden, 1971.

Han M. M. Fortmann, *Oosterse Renaissance*. Bilthoven, 1970.

———, *Heel de Mens*. Bilthoven, 1972.

H. T. de Graaf, *Om het eeuwig Goed*. Arnhem, 1923.

———, *De Godsdienst in het Licht der Zielkunde*. Assen, 1928.

Abel J. Herzberg, *Brieven aan mijn Kleinzoon*, 's-Gravenhage, 1964.

L. van der Hortse, *Psychopathologie en Mensbeschouwing*. Amsterdam, 1946.

Ursula Lehr, *Psychologie des Alterns*. Heidelberg, 1977.

Bernard Lievegoed, *De Levensloop van de Mens*. Rotterdam, 1977.

Jan Matse, *Het laatste Kwartier*. Meppel, 1977.

J. M. A. Munnichs, *Ouderdom en Eindigheid*. Assen, 1964.

———, *Bouwstenen voor een sociale Gerontologie*. Nijmegen, 1972.

A. Polspoel, *Wenen om het verloren Ik*. Hilversum, 1979.

H. C. Rümke, *Levenstijdperken van de Man*. Amsterdam, 1938.

———, *Studies en Voordrachten over Psychiatrie*. Amsterdam, 1943.

A. A. A. Terruwe, *Geloven zonder Angst en Vrees*. Roermond, 1970.

Eduard Spranger, *Psychologie des Jugendalters*. Leipzig, 1925.

Erich Stern, *Der Mensch in der zweiten Lebenshälfte*. Zürich, 1955.

A. L. Vischer, *Seelische Wandlungen beim alternden Menschen*. Basel, 1949.